Encouraging Your Child's
Writing Talent

Encouraging Your Child's
Writing Talent
The Involved Parents' Guide

Nancy **Peterson, Ed.D.**

Prufrock Press Inc.
Waco, Texas

Library of Congress Cataloging-in-Publication Data

Peterson, Nancy L.
  Encouraging your child's writing talent : the involved parents' guide / by Nancy L. Peterson.
    p. cm.
  Includes bibliographical references.
  ISBN 1-59363-185-5 (pbk.)
  1. English language—Composition and exercises. 2. Children—Writing. 3. Education—
Parent participation. I. Title.
  LB1576.P5514 2006
  372.62'3—dc22
                        2005037610

Edited by Lacy Elwood, Cover design by Marjorie Parker, Layout design by Kim Worley

ISBN-13: 978-1-59363-185-7
ISBN-10: 1-59363-185-5

Printed in the United States of America.

Excerpt on pages 78–79 reprinted by permission from *Writing Workshop: The Essential Guide* by
Ralph Fletcher and JoAnn Portalupi. Copyright ©2001 by Ralph Fletcher and JoAnn Portalupi.
Published by Heinemann, a division of Reed Elsevier, Inc., Portsmouth, NH. All rights reserved.

At the time of this book's publication, all facts and figures cited are the most current available. All
telephone numbers, addresses, and Web site URLs are accurate and active. All publications, organizations, Web sites, and other resources exist as described in the book, and all have been verified.
The authors and Prufrock Press Inc., make no warranty or guarantee concerning the information
and materials given out by organizations or content found at Web sites, and we are not responsible for any changes that occur after this book's publication. If you find an error, please contact
Prufrock Press Inc. We strongly recommend to parents, teachers, and other adults that you moni-
tor children's use of the Internet.

PRUFROCK PRESS INC.
P.O. BOX 8813
Waco, Texas 76714-8813
(800) 998-2208
http://www.prufrock.com

To Happy, Sundy, Lacey, and Paul, my children and my teachers.

Contents

— Chapter **1** —
Your Child—A Writer   7

— Chapter **2** —
What Your Child Needs as a Writer   37

— Chapter **3** —
Working With the School to Encourage Your Child as a Writer   61

— Chapter **4** —
What You Can Do at Home for Your Gifted Writer   85

— Chapter **5** —
Enrichment Resources for Your Young Writer   123

Conclusion: Writing and Flying   151

References   157
About the Author   161

—List of **Tables & Figures**—

Introduction

…writing is not a performance but a generosity.
—Brenda Ueland, 1938

Writing: That powerful tool that is more than a tool, the device that transcends the mere passing of a message from one to another, the instrument that can bring men and women to tears or to action for a cause, an implement of joy and pleasure to human beings that conveys hope and ignites love, laughter, and tears.

At the time of this writing, publicized responses to the new timed writing components that have recently been added to the SAT and ACT college entrance exams are just beginning to surface. The National Council of Teachers of English (NCTE; 2005) just released the following statement: "To say that writing is a process is decidedly not to say that it should—or can—be turned into a formulaic set of steps. Experienced writers shift between different operations according to tasks and circumstances" (p. 1).

According to NCTE, effective writing is learned in many different situations, and this portion of the college entrance exams could limit the range of writing that is taught in schools. This is one more hit on responsive and reflective teaching that has been gravely endangered in this day of high stakes test-driven classroom practices. Good young writers may well become an endangered commodity.

On the surface, writing is marking on a page for a purpose, usually to express an idea or to communicate information through print. We are indebted to ancient civilizations who devised symbols and systems that gave written markings the power of thought and intent. Writing is the intentional selection of specific words, putting them to a surface in a particular order. *Good* writing transcends the formation of letters and words in a particular order on a page, and can move us to emotion, response, or action. Writing is talk on paper. Talk is how literature began. For centuries before humans wrote, they told stories and passed information along orally. Even when they began to write, the flavor of oral interchange remained. Good writers, then, are able to communicate purpose, emotion, truth, or some combination of these to the reader. Those who learn to write well truly have one of the most powerful tools imaginable, and because good writing is so closely connected to the mind and heart, it is a talent that can powerfully impact others, as well as ourselves.

> Those who learn to write well truly have one of the most powerful tools imaginable, and because good writing is so closely connected to the mind and heart, it is a talent that can powerfully impact others...

Those who write for their livelihoods share something that seems somewhat undefinable, but far from intangible. It seems that writers' souls are interconnected by golden threads; that they are frequent visitors to a river of words that flows freely through the landscape of their lives. How do we assist those we love most to observe this landscape, describe what they see, and jump in?

How can we facilitate their development of the capacity to write for powerful public and personal reasons that surpass timed writing skills tested in schools, and to use writing to empower themselves in reaching their own highest potential?

The written word is essential to our very lives. The practical details of our everyday living demand at least a perfunctory aptitude in writing. In the beginning, students depend on learning about and using the written word in order to survive and succeed. This reliance on the ability to write, and the need for proficiency in it increases through the years as children assimilate information about the world around them, and demonstrate their growing knowledge and understandings. Learning to write well at an early age helps tremendously when, in the middle and high school years, the levels of writing assignments increase to crucial stages. But, more importantly, the development of our children's values, ideas, and dreams merit an equally incisive and fitting means of communication.

As Langston Hughes said of James Baldwin, the 20th century African American author,

> [He] writes down to nobody, and he is trying very hard to write up to himself. As an essayist he is thought-provoking, tantalizing, irritating, abusing and amusing. And he uses words as the sea uses waves, to flow and beat, advance and retreat, rise and take a bow in disappearing. (Hughes, 1958, ¶ 1)

Some children—perhaps your child among them—are ready to embark upon this voyage. We—their parents—can help them navigate those waves.

As the Sea Uses Waves

The oldest of nine children, James Baldwin grew up in an impoverished area of Harlem. Even as a child, he desperately sought for an escape from his circumstances, which were worsened by a troubled relationship with his strict stepfather. Recognizing his own intelligence, James found the public library to be a place where he could retreat with his mind. Even as a child, Baldwin was a voracious reader who became a writer. His first story appeared in a church newspaper when he was about 12 years old. By the time he was 14, Baldwin had discovered his passion for writing, and he began seriously studying writing and writers at about age 19.

During his lifetime, he produced a number of important works of literature, and by the time of his death in 1987, Baldwin had become one of the most important advocates of equality in America, and had published works that remain essential parts of the American canon, including *Go Tell It On the Mountain, The Evidence of Things Not Seen,* and *Notes of a Native Son.* Did writing make a difference in his life? Was it a benefit to him as a child? Beginning as a reader and becoming a writer made *all* the difference for James Baldwin, and thousands of others through the years, including those who have read his books.

Children possess creative power and an innate propensity for their writing to make a difference in the world. We can inspire the desire to do so by sharing with them the books that have done that for us. In a letter responding to the question, "What book made the greatest difference in your life?," the late actor Walter Matthau wrote:

The book that made the greatest difference in my life was *The Secret in the Daisy,* by Carol Grace, Random House, published 1955. The difference it made was enormous.

It took me from a miserable, unhappy wretch to a joyful, glad-to-be-alive human. I fell so in love with the book that I searched out and married the girl who wrote it. (as cited in Sabine & Sabine, 1983, p. 29)

At the very least, children can make a difference in their own lives through writing.

Children can write but someone has to *tell* them they can do it. Someone has to apprise them of their wonderful ideas and entice their talents forward—to position them to ride that wave of possibility. Teachers, parents, and peers can each play a part in the process. Parents, in particular, can explore the extraordinary opportunity of guiding their children to that sea of expression, communication, and understanding. Parents can lead their children to the tremendous power within, and show their children how "writing is an outlet for [their] creative expression, a way of transmitting the scenes inside [their] heads to the world at large . . . " (Cramer, 2001, p. xiii).

Written language takes years to master. Yet, in spite of all of its conventions and complexities, it must have a beginning. There is a place for each child to begin a journey on a river of words. When children are given a good beginning, there really is no limit to where their writing can take them.

Chapter 1

Your Child—A Writer

Creative children look twice, listen for smells, dig deeper, build dream castles, get from behind locked doors, have a ball, plug in the sun, get into and out of deep water, sing in their own key.
—Paul Torrance, 1973

I n Antoine de Saint-Exupery's *The Little Prince* (1971), we, with the Prince, learn that "what is essential is invisible to the eye"; that it is "only with the heart that [we] can see rightly" (p. 87). Good writers are able to go beyond spelling, grammar, and coherency to make the invisible visible. Gifted writers have more than an average ability to communicate with clarity, to write with technical ease, and/or to express deep emotion. They can meaningfully communicate in ways that surpass conventional patterns or strings of words on a page. Their heightened ability to communicate exceeds the typical development of the rote skill of writing, and becomes integrated and enmeshed with higher order thinking and in-depth manipulation of ideas, eliciting in us aesthetic, intellectual, emotional, or visceral responses. Gifted writing causes us to open our hearts wide for the information, messages, and stories.

In *The Neglected "R": The Need for a Writing Revolution* (College Board, 2003), a report by the College Board's National Commission on Writing, we are told that writing, at its best,

> . . . has helped transform the world. Revolutions have been started by it.
>
> Oppression has been toppled by it. And it has enlightened the human condition. American life has been richer because people like Rachel Carson, César Chávez, Thomas Jefferson, and Martin Luther King, Jr. have given voice to the aspirations of the nation and its people. And it has become fuller because writers like James Baldwin, William Faulkner, Toni Morrison, and Edith Wharton have explored the range of human misery and joy. (p. 10)

Our children may be destined to add their voices to these ranks. What will motivate us to care about the human existence of our future? Who will inspire us to understand, recall, or connect new ideas with wisdom of the ages? In their capacity as writers, our children may well be those to document the greatest discoveries yet. Whether or not your child competes for the Pulitzer Prize, he will, throughout his life, be writing to inform; to record, define, and explain; to condense, summarize, and interpret; to teach; to persuade; to prompt, amuse, or inspire; and generally, to make sense of this changing world. True writing begins with listening. Knowing how to open the heart of a reader can fulfill the life and purpose of a writer. Even young children are capable of meaningful communication experiences, and some signs of an advanced penchant to be a writer are noticeable in emergent and beginning writing. We just have to know what to look for, how to see it, and how to inspire or encourage it.

Fulfilling our children's lives and purposes as writers is to allow and encourage them to write about what they care about, for causes that move or inspire them. As my 16-year-old son learns to drive, I am reminded that no one is motivated to become a good driver by learning *about* driving. Would-be drivers are not inspired by learning how to position the rear-view mirrors, or learning the facts of how many lives are saved by the proper use of seatbelts. Would-be drivers are inspired by their experiences in watching others drive by in nice cars, and by envisioning themselves behind the wheel, confidently gliding toward a desired destination. As real driving becomes a more realistic possibility through practice driving with a learner's permit and a driving instructor, the importance of the rear-view mirror and seatbelt safety automatically take on their proper priority. The process of real driving makes all the little parts of learning to drive significant and personally meaningful.

This also is true for becoming a good writer. The ideas that fill our children's minds and the stories that whisper to their hearts must be told in order to make all of the separate skills significant and personally meaningful. For some children, there is meaning and truth literally locked inside their minds, waiting for the right key to open the door to something they will love for the rest of their lives. Writers are fulfilled when they write the stories their hearts need to tell. The writing process can be outlined simply as the writer choosing his topic, deciding on his purpose, targeting a desired audience, taking his time to draft and redraft, talking over his writing with others he trusts, and, if he is lucky and still interested, publishing his creation. In determining if a child has the ability or gift for writing, do we help her discover those ideas and stories, or do we give her the skills and let her find the ideas and stories for herself?

Teaching children how to write is hard, because writing is a whole array of multiple skills rather than just one skill. This array of writing skills includes creating, sequencing, spelling, categorizing and organizing, rereading, and supporting big ideas with examples. These subskills are developmental, and they *can* be learned. In fact, most children absent of debilitating learning problems do eventually learn, figure out, and practice writing to some extent. Traditionally, the ability to pass a test and to produce some specific piece of writing has been the ultimate goal of learning to write. In the classroom, the writing process has all too often been the teachers' means to those ends—passing tests and completing products. However, overemphasis on product is destructive to good writing, and can whip the gift and the desire for it right out of some children's lives. Many traditional approaches to teaching writing focus on correctness and drilling of skills to the detriment of content.

On the other hand, overemphasis on the process of writing (just writing to write), can undervalue correctness and skill to the detriment of a good and desirable written product. Offering motivation or inspiration for children's writing without empowering them with knowledge and ability can be a detriment to a natural development of an enjoyable and powerful tool. Overemphasis of the process can prevent the completion of products that reward the writer's process. Overemphasis of *either* process or product as more important than the other is unhealthy. However, it is clear to mentors with a great deal of experience managing the writing process and reading thousands of pages of others' writing products, that valuing good ideas is more important than correctly expressing mundane ones. Children deserve what writer Ralph Fletcher calls "honesty tempered by compassion." He states, "Our words will literally define the ways they perceive themselves as writers" (1993, p. 19).

Parents who wish to mentor their child's writing life should hope to do more than hone their child's conventional expression of ideas with pen to paper or fingers to keyboard. Our mentorship as parents should be more about discovery than judgment, more about fluency than technique, and more about mentoring than assigning. Writing is learned through writing, reading, and perceiving oneself as a writer. Writing teachers must gain an understanding of what a child faces in learning to write. We must develop in ourselves a vision that will inspire our child-writers to think, speak, and plan like the writers whose prose and poetry they love, and whose books we buy. We can, with our young writers, learn to look at their writing with intense curiosity and desire for understanding as we clear a path for them on their journey to opening hearts wide—ours, their own, and others'.

> Our mentorship as parents should be more about discovery than judgment, more about fluency than technique, and more about mentoring than assigning.

Recognizing Writing Ability in Your Child

Children who are or have the innate potential to be gifted writers usually display considerable imagination. They may readily come up with unique stories, either spontaneously, or in a more drawn-out process. Their creativity may be manifested in many ways, but it will be particularly apparent in verbal expressiveness. They may show remarkable facial or physical expressiveness, use fascinating vocabulary, and be drawn to read and reread (or repeatedly listen to) vivid descriptions in books and stories.

You may come to recognize innate ability for writing when you notice your child exhibiting some combination of the char-

---

Table 1
Characteristics of Gifted Writers

- tell stories or relate events with great detail and expression
- develop some system of organizing thoughts to make sense of the world
- are fascinated by words, letters, and sounds
- exhibit a playfulness with language
- convey distinctly personal voice in their writings
- find the act of seeing their ideas in print irresistible
- love to draw, and do so with more than average detail for age and experience
- attempt to connect their ideas to others' ideas
- write more and more coherently than peers of the same age
- display a deep desire for the listener or reader to feel something about or because of what they have written

---

acteristics listed in Table 1 and discussed in detail in the next few sections. Many of these same characteristics and behaviors have been noted in writers' group discussions, and in dialogue between successful writers and published authors. Some of these innate characteristics have been notably present early in the memories of numerous published authors.

Characteristics of Gifted Writers

Your child may tell stories or relate events with great detail and expression. Most of us are storytellers. We are constantly telling each other about our lives—what happened to us, what we saw, what we thought. We share news of dramatic events in our lives and in the lives of our friends. We repeat jokes we have heard; we share dreams and memories. Watch children in any group setting where they are invited to share a comment or a connection to the

Kindergarten child A: "The dentist pulled my first tooth."   Kindergarten child B: "I got a metal tooth."

Figure 1. Lost tooth stories

discussion topic. Children rarely want to stop sharing, and many a preschool or kindergarten teacher has lost control of an organized group discussion, and of her own reactions to the delightfully innocent observations depicted by the children. The desire to tell something begins very early for most children, much earlier than their ability to write down their thoughts.

However, detailed verbal explanations and questions—even some early humor, as well as animated verbal and physical expressions with which some children share their news or ideas—can be motivation to attempt documentation of their words in writing. This willingness to put their words in print, including details that are important to them, may be very distinguishable signs of a propensity to write well. In Figure 1, we can see two descriptions of losing teeth, written by two different kindergartners. The writing topic was inspired by the discussion that followed one girl's announcement that she had just lost her first tooth over the weekend. Every child then had a story to tell, and many of them were willing to write their stories down.

A first-grade teacher who holds regular morning meetings (open discussion about child-selected topics) and a daily writing workshop, asked her students to write a letter to someone. One little girl's letter, at first glance, actually worried the teacher, until she got to the end (see Figure 2 on p. 15).

The teacher recognized the true intended recipient of this letter, a bruise on Elena's leg, because of the illustration. This little writer is already playing with the concept of personification. Notice that she is not concerned about every convention of writing in her draft, but demonstrates some sophisticated guessing by dividing the word *made* into "ma-de" at the end of the line.

Your child may develop some system of organizing thoughts to make sense of his or her world. Innately able writers somehow give shape and focus to their ideas. Some like to talk, or ask questions, or have questions asked of them. Children will usually become comfortable with one or more of these thought processes. They may enjoy drawing a picture and then explaining it in great detail. Many children rehearse thoughts in their minds before they speak out. They may think about how to begin, what to say next, and how and when to end their verbal thought or retelling. They may sometimes forget to verbalize some step in that thought process. Wise teachers and parents will not dismiss comments that seem to have no connection to the topic being discussed. I have admired teachers who respond with something like, "I've never thought of it like that before. How did you think of that?" When my children were young, an acquaintance pointed out that he had heard my husband on several occasions asking our children, "Where did you get this idea? Please tell me about this."

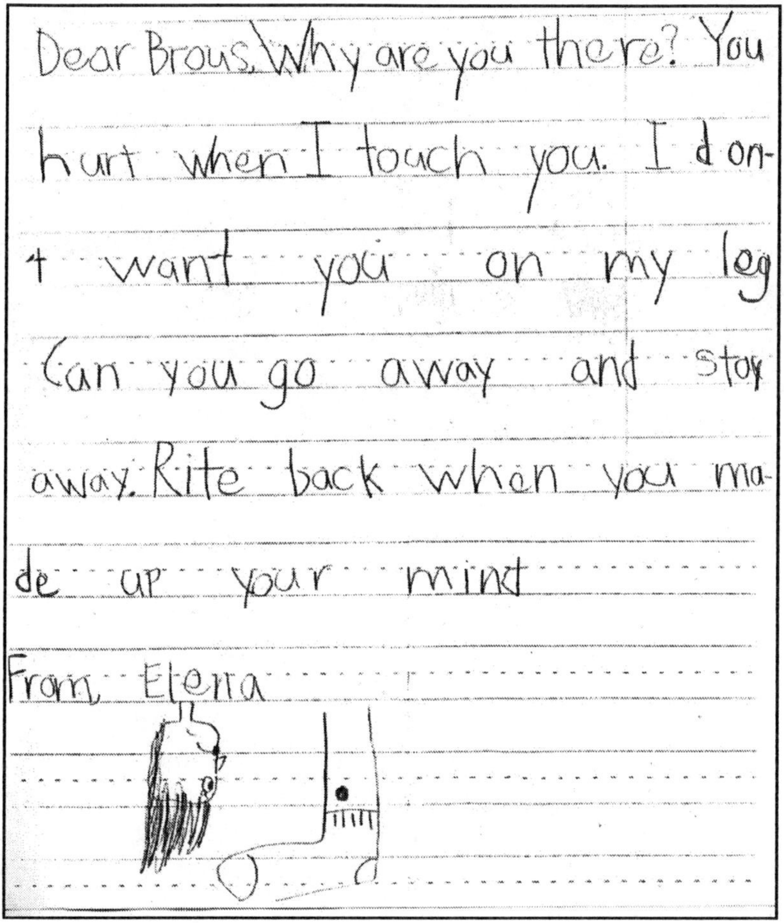

Dear Brous. Why are you there? You hurt when I touch you. I don't want you on my leg. Can you go away and stay away. Rite back when you made up your mind.

From, Elena

"Dear Bruise, Why are you there? You hurt when I touch you. I don't want you on my leg. Can you go away and stay away? Write back when you made up your mind. From, Elena."

Figure 2. Letter from a first grader

Wonderful and purposeful discussions occur in groups of young children where the adult honors the children's thinking

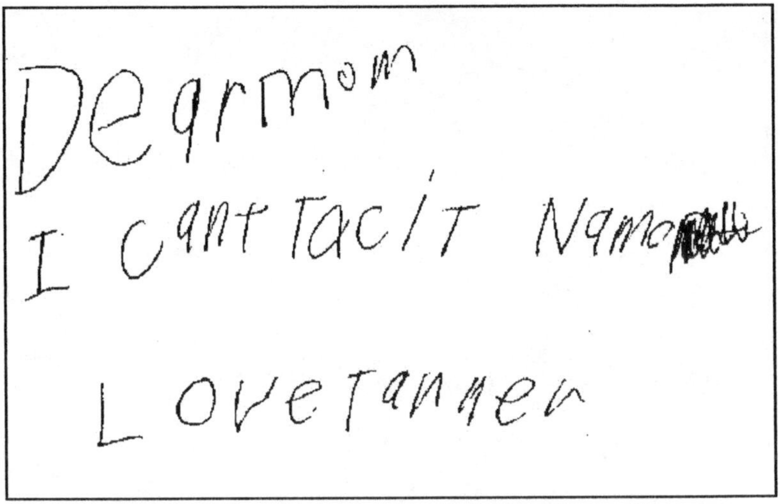

"Dear Mom, I can't take it any more. Love, Tanner."

Figure 3. A note from a kindergarten student

processes, even beyond what seems to make sense when first spoken. One of my students found out firsthand the strength of a child's thought process. After multiple grueling sessions helping her 5-year-old son complete his reading and writing exercises (kindergarten homework), my student found a note on her pillow (see Figure 3). Her son composed and drafted the note in his invented spelling and new mode of expression, all by himself.

Innate writers may become fascinated by words, letters, and sounds. An acquaintance of mine bought an illustrated dictionary for her 7-year-old granddaughter. The little girl carries the dictionary with her everywhere she goes. She copies entire lists of words from her dictionary. She writes notes to her friends and family members, always referring to the dictionary for new words to include in her notes. She reads long strings of words from several dictionary pages in a row, and giggles about how some of the words sound to her, or how some of the sounds *feel* when she says them.

While some children whose writing ability is just emerging will go to great lengths to find the proper spelling of a word they *must* use in their writing, because they have heard or seen the word somewhere else, other children are determined to get their message across with the right words, regardless of their lack of knowledge about the conventional spelling. Even a child's invented spellings of relatively sophisticated vocabulary can reveal a rather sophisticated experimentation with sounds *before* the child is actually able to recognize and remember the conventional spellings. When a child writes a complex word, even if it is misspelled, it may be worth noting how he or she perceives the spelling that has prompted its use. Teachers often observe that children's naïve use of complicated language reflects the levels of their listening comprehension levels. This is a particular source of humor for first- and second-grade teachers after they've endured 30 minutes of short writer's conferences and answered numerous "Teacher, how do you spell . . . ?" requests in the writing period.

I observed the passing of notes between two first graders who were presumably imitating some movie dialogue. One of the 6-year-old girls wrote, "He was jrivn to love me." Her use of a phrase such as "driven to love me" was a rather humorous attempt at sophistication in the first place. But, when you add the observation of her using "jrivn" as the spelling for driven, you notice her attention to all of the sounds that are present in the word, and a deliberate willingness to chance a guess at spelling it in order to use what she believes is just the right word. A child who feels compelled to use just the right word for every occasion will soon learn the correct spellings of the words she wants to use.

It is important to remember that from the ages of 5–8, children's inventive spellings can more accurately be called "temporary spelling." The important element here is not the correct spelling upon first drafting the use of interesting and fascinating words, but the fact that this interest will lead to an interest and fascination with the conventional spellings. Words that have personal meaning to a writer are words that will inspire a writer to seek conventional knowledge. Oh, that our children may feel the freedom to thirst for new words! Poet Georgia Heard (1995) understands this personal connection; she loves words and language even today:

> I haunt used-book stores, searching for books that contain unusual words. *Elementary Seamanship* has a glossary of sea terms: *scupper, bulwark, winch, windlass, scuttles.* The book is a cup of possibility for those days when I'm thirsty for words. (p. 47)

Your child may exhibit a playfulness with language. An example of playfulness with language in an early writer can be seen in Figure 4.

This first-grade author discovered, while she was writing her draft—the first ideas that came to her mind—that she could write a lot of words by describing her topic with first a rhyme (bug hug), and then a list of all the family words she knew. It was apparent that she liked what she had written when she read her words out loud and discovered there was a little rhythm in there, as well. That discovery led her to immediately share her new poem with her teacher.

Rick Walton, prolific author of picture books that feature a playful use of language and parts of speech, credits an eighth-grade teacher with inspiring his enjoyment of words. The teacher held a contest for creating the longest list of compound words—the winner would have lunch with a local college basketball celeb-

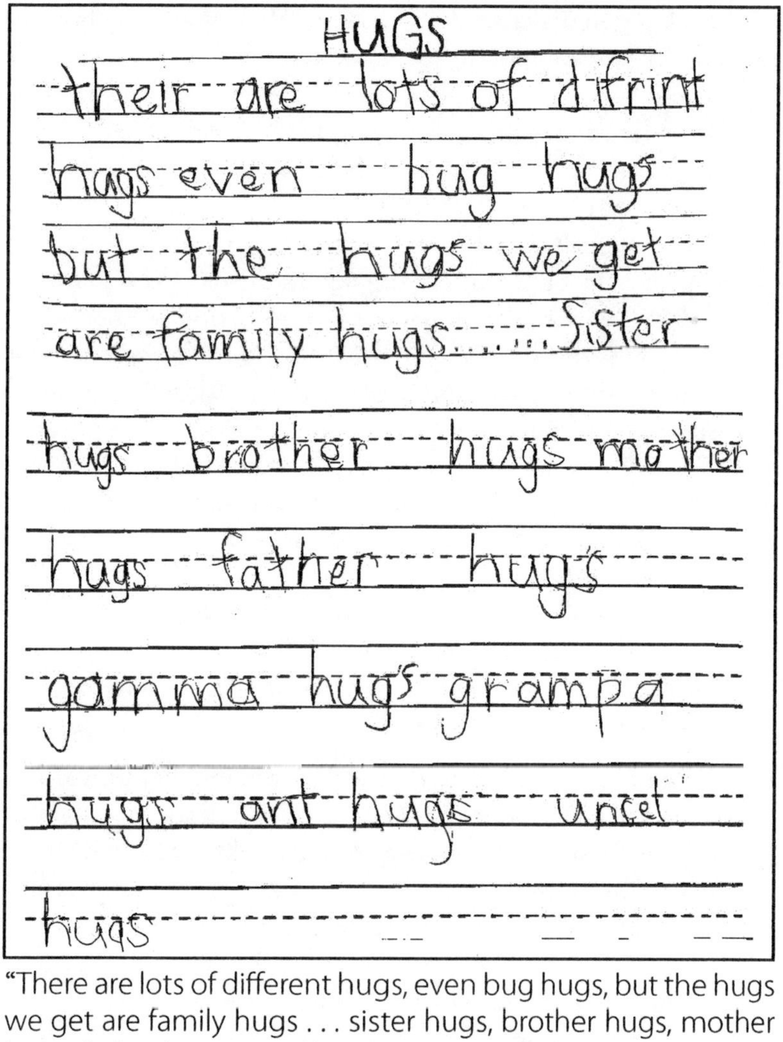

HUGS

their are lots of difrint hugs even bug hugs but the hugs we get are family hugs...... sister hugs brother hugs mother hugs father hug's gamma hug's grampa hugs ant hugs uncel hugs

"There are lots of different hugs, even bug hugs, but the hugs we get are family hugs . . . sister hugs, brother hugs, mother hugs, father hugs, grandma hugs, grandpa hugs, aunt hugs, uncle hugs."

Figure 4. Playing with words

rity. Rick began searching for compound words, and his final list included 1,500 compound words, written by hand on a stack of papers. He says it was easy for him, as he recognized that he loves words. "I loved playing with words. I loved reading words, and writing words, and studying words, and finding out interesting facts about words" (Walton, 2003, ¶ 4).

Rick has built that love of wordplay into a successful career writing picture books, including *Once There Was a Bull . . . frog* (1997), which plays with compound words. Other books include *Why the Banana Split* (1998), which presents synonyms and idioms, and *Bullfrog Pops!* (1999), which features transitive and intransitive verbs and direct objects. These, along with Walton's many other books, demonstrate the influence of his early and ongoing love for and clever play with language, and have become favorites of elementary teachers and students alike.

Mem Fox, whose mother was an English teacher and whose father was a minister, also relies on wordplay in her writings. Fox (1993) tells of how the language of the Bible and of Shakespeare influenced her writing and speaking:

> The sonorousness, position of words, the number of words per phrase, the rhythms of those phrases, and the placement of the pauses have been collected in a storehouse from which I draw constantly, particularly for opening and closing sentences. Listening to the Bible developed my need to read aloud every sentence I write in order to check its balance and meaning. When I read or write, I hear. The words I've read ring in my ears and reverberate against the ceilings of my storehouse, echoing their way into my own writing. (p. 31)

Your child's writing may convey distinctly unique personal voice. Personal voice is when your child's personality shines through his writing, and noticing voice is akin to recognizing your child's individuality in what he says and how he says it. Some elements of voice in writing, such as connecting with an audience, can be taught and developed as strategies. But, other elements, such as honesty, confidence, or humor, may emerge early or in their own time, and must be invited, valued, applauded, and nurtured. In *Creating Writers Through 6-Trait Writing*, Vicki Spandel (2005b) says,

> Voice is many things: personality, passion, engagement with the topic, energy and enthusiasm, and audience sensitivity. Because voice builds a bridge from writer to reader, it is much more than a fancy accoutrement; it is a tool for ensuring that the reader pays attention to the message. Voice connects us to the text. (p. 93)

Letting one's voice come through in writing takes courage, and therefore will likely occur when your child feels safe in writing down her personal truth and in sharing it aloud. I do not mean *truth* as defined by literal facts. I mean truth as your child sees it and as it encompasses her response to the world; what she sees and believes deep inside. Ralph Fletcher (1993) believes that the best environments for writing with voice are where children can "put themselves on the line when they write" (p. 26). As a teacher, I work hard to develop recognition of my students' unique voices in their writing. As a parent of a young writer, you will want to try to recognize how your child's voice in describing a given event differs from his peers' voices in their writing about the same or similar events.

Some experts on the development of writing have suggested that the courage required of a child to let his or her voice come through is one possible hallmark of extraordinary inclination for writing ability. Donald Murray (1985) has said that voice is the quality, "more than any other, that allows us to hear exceptional potential" in a beginning writer (p. 21). Authors often speak of their own writing in terms of their "craft," and the writing craft most often discussed in their presentations is that of voice. They recognize it in each other's writing, and they are thrilled when they skillfully achieve it in their own writing. It may be that your child's desire to *feel* unique motivates her to write in a noticeably unique way—in a voice that is all her own.

Your child may find the act of writing and seeing his or her own ideas in print irresistible. A young writer with an innate talent for writing will usually possess an urge to write that is unrelated or unaffected by others' evaluations and judgments of his or her work. Writers just seem to know, often very early on, that they *have* to write! If your child has not had much opportunity to see his own writing in print, or you haven't yet recognized his craving for it, you may be able to recognize this characteristic when you give him a writer's notebook and the freedom to use it as he chooses.

> A young writer with an innate talent for writing will usually possess an urge to write that is unrelated or unaffected by others' evaluations and judgments of his or her work. Writers just seem to know, often very early on, that they have to write!

One of my former students, Emily, is a writer who recently began teaching fifth grade. Emily purchased little notebooks for each of her students, and shared with them often what she wrote in her own writer's notebook. Emily discovered one child who could not observe, think about, or write *enough* to satisfy himself. Through his teacher's guidance and through other writing that she introduced to the class, he began to do what real writers do— keep a notebook full of ideas and inspiration. Emily admitted that without the writer's notebook experiences of this student, she would not have discovered the boy's gift for and compulsion to write. Much of it unrecognizable, the student's writing pre-

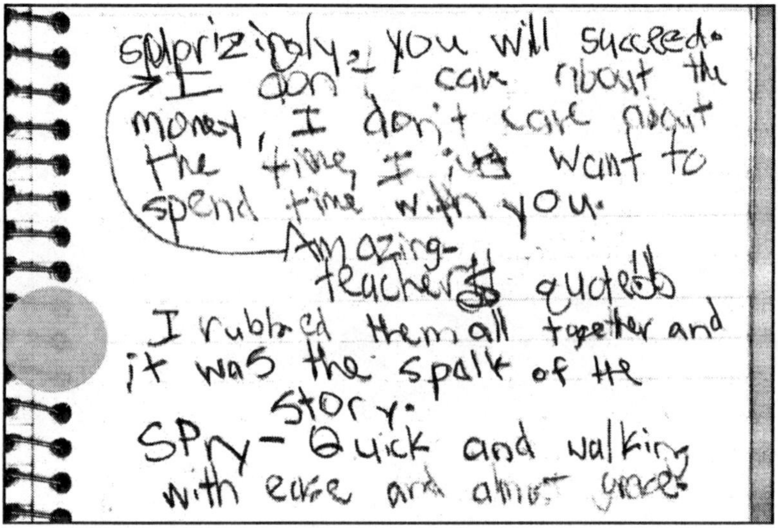

"Surprisingly, you will succeed. I don't care about the money, I don't care about the time, I just want to spend time with you. Amazing—Teacher's quote!! I rubbed them all together and it was the spark of the story. Spry—quick and walking with ease and almost grace."

Figure 5. An excerpt from Nate's writing notebook

viously had been judged as sloppy and unreadable by teachers. The freedom to write in his own notebook without the constant scrutiny of a teacher prompted prolific writing. The pages of his writer's notebook are full of spelling and grammar problems, and admittedly, some illegible writing. But, the content is rich. His pages are full of amazing observations he has made, experimentations with words and phrases he has heard, and attempts at first drafts of purposeful writing products. Figure 5 includes some of his entries in his writing notebook. This 11-year-old boy is a writer!

Figure 6. Markell's drawing

Your child may love to draw, and do so with more than average detail for his or her age and experience. If your child loves to draw, and draws often and a lot, and if she pays close attention to creating meticulous details in her drawings, she will easily and naturally channel that same creativity and attention to detail in her writing. Your child may readily tell a story about the drawings, or may demonstrate an ability to do so upon your invitation. Seven-year-old Markell has not yet found comfort in her use of the printed word. In fact, her mother has been worried that Markell may have a mild learning disability. But, Markell does compose many detailed stories and situations in her drawings. In Figure 6, Markell explained to her mother verbally that the figure in the middle of the foreground is a groundhog coming out of his hole. She elaborated, "But, he runs back in, not because he sees his shadow. It's because he is scared of all the lights and cameras set up around his hole."

The process of drawing with detail is very similar to the process of composing words in writing. When this interest in detailed drawing is acknowledged, encouraged, and nurtured, it will likely develop into the ability to write well as the subskills of writing are learned and mastered. This characteristic of drawing in great detail may actually be initial attempts to reveal some type of emotion about something. Figure 7 (see page 26) was produced in response to a teacher's instructions for second graders to draw a picture of her—the teacher. The tiger in the forefront and the snake slithering up the tree in this "portrait" may reveal something adversarial about this 7-year-old boy's perception of the kind of role this teacher played in his life. The 23 other portraits displayed on the classroom wall included only the teacher, and mostly just her head.

Some teachers are bothered by a child who draws pictures all over his homework pages or class worksheets. More often than not, these kinds of drawings are full of rich detail, and supported by well-developed, but unspoken stories or chunks of reasoning. I have observed that doodling in patterns or random marks does not typically occur until one's late teenage or young adult years. I have rarely seen mindless doodles on younger children's papers, but I have seen many detailed drawings. I strongly recommend that parents and teachers observe children's drawings closely, and ask questions or give your child opportunities to describe or explain the drawings before dismissing them.

My 16-year-old son drew all over his primary grade assignments. He often was careless in the tasks required on the worksheets, but more than adequately detailed in his drawings on the same worksheets. Most of his drawings had a theme of piles of space rocks and a specific little reoccurring character. He is now

Figure 7. The teacher

writing and illustrating an original fantasy trilogy, which he began when he was 14. Both details from those childhood drawings, space rocks and the little character, appear in his current attempt at serious writing—first symbolically, and later as major themes.

In his speaking engagements, Christopher Bing, who won a Caldecott Honor award for his book, *Casey at the Bat: A Ballad of the Republic Sung in the Year 1888* (published in 2000), has said that he has doodled all over his papers since he was a young child. He loved drawing and he loved stories. As an adult author and illustrator, he has created some beautiful children's books.

As children, innately able writers may continually attempt to connect their own ideas to others' ideas. You may notice that your child is constantly connecting her own new ideas to her older ideas. She may verbally express these connections, or spend a great deal of time writing them down. She may volunteer her ideas in discussions as examples of what she understands or believes about the discussion topic. This suggests more of a thinking style or intellectual development than progress of writing ability, and is consistent with the earliest developmental stages that occurred in early childhood. As your child travels along the typical developmental stages in physical, emotional, and mental aspects, he also acquires thought structures, learning strategies, and language. Table 2 describes several developmental theories. Language becomes instrumental in directing his thinking and learning, and the richer his language becomes, the more unstinted is his intellectual development.

Your child's discovery of his own ability to connect new thoughts and ideas with old ones is an exciting validation of his own intellect. So is the discovery that he can connect his own thoughts with the thoughts and ideas of others. Even an early curiosity about words and their meanings, with subsequent use in his language or writing is a sign of this development of thinking ability. Interactive discussions about words do occur between children and adults, as was apparent during a visit to a kindergar-

Table 2
Developmental Learning and Language Theories

The following developmental psychologists are among the most influential theorists of the 20th century. While each theorist's ideas were distinctly different from the others', they proposed related ideas about the interaction of language and intellectual development.

Theorist	Proposals	Application for Development of Writing
Jean Piaget	• Language acquisition is stimulated by thinking. • Thinking is stimulated by children's actions upon the concrete world. • Children develop language in order to label their concrete experiences and observations. • Language transmits thinking; it also refines and elaborates on thinking.	• Provide experiences that allow children to physically and socially experiment with writing materials. • Use the arts and play in group and individual settings to motivate lots of language use. • Encourage children to actively participate often in real-world events and discuss them so that language and experience seem to fit together naturally.
Lev Vygotsky	• Children gain understanding and meaning through their exposure to adults as they model the use of language.	• Stress social interaction with adults and peers to broaden their experiences. • Work cooperatively with children through

Table 2, continued		
Theorist	Proposals	Application for Development of Writing
Lev Vygotsky, continued	• Concrete experiences with objects, accompanied by simultaneous encounters with language provide the framework through which children's thinking develops. • Children learn best when they are in the zone of proximal development, the point of entry or level of readiness where they are most receptive of interaction and guidance from an adult.	sharing, think-aloud modeling, and one-on-one discussions about writing. • Listen, speak, question, and chat with children to model language through interaction.
Jerome Bruner	• Children learn to think abstractly through their use of language. • Interactive conversations with adults motivate children to learn to examine, structure, and reflect on their experiences.	• Stress active experimentation and interaction with ideas and in environments that are familiar and meaningful to children. • Make the most of the natural relationship between talking and writing in multiple settings.

Table 2, continued		
Theorist	Proposals	Application for Development of Writing
Jerome Bruner, continued	• The strategies children learn during language acquisition are useful for other development of their thinking. • Children learn best through discovery learning and problem solving	• Create or make use of learning centers or museum displays, independent reading (and pretend reading in preliterate stages), propose problems to solve for fun, and use computers and other educational games.

Note. Compiled from Bruner, 1966; Piaget, 1955; and Vygotsky, 1962.

ten classroom. The kindergarten student teacher scolded a little boy for tearing up a picture that had been drawn by the little girl sitting next to him. "This is *not* acceptable!" exclaimed the student teacher, holding the torn pieces of paper in front of the boy. The little boy looked at the student teacher with a perplexed expression for several silent moments. Finally the boy responded, "I'm going to have to go home and ask my dad about that word—acceptable."

Environments where open discussion and exchange of ideas are encouraged and engaged in often will produce the occasional discovery that a child has thinking and writing abilities that may not have been realized before. Teachers and parents should be inspired by this discovery, but the children themselves should be delighted by the self-discovery, as well. The confidence this creates is what we often notice about intellectually gifted kids. Naysayers may chalk this up to the child being overtly and inappropriately verbal, or simply liking to "hear herself talk." However, when this pattern has occurred, we should take notice and look into possible outlets for this self-discovery of intellectual understanding. How is this intellectual development related to writing? It actually inspires and nourishes the desire to write, and the inner drive of the child to improve and sharpen his writing skills. He wants the world to know about the connections he's making.

A child who keeps and writes in her own private journal on a regular basis, even after a school journal assignment has ended, may be keeping ongoing connections to things she has seen, read, or heard, and sharing thoughts, stories, or comparisons to other literature in her journal. Nate began keeping a journal in fifth grade after his teacher, Emily Konold, presented thinking strategies that she and other authors use. Every few days Nate excitedly shared with Emily his journal entries and compositions that were based on the connections he made while writing in his journal. Over time, Emily noticed that Nate's journal entries included snippets of Emily's stories, words and phrases, and written observations similar to the ones Emily had shared with the class.

Nate was obviously connecting his thoughts with the thoughts of others. He wrote down the words of his teacher, phrases from literature she read aloud to the class, and descriptions of his observations of the world around him. Later in the year, Nate began sharing poetry he had written (unassigned) based on entries in his journal. One example of Nate's poetry and its connection to his journal can be found in Figure 8. This was a powerful insight for Emily that Nate was displaying an extraordinary ability to make and document connections to others' thoughts, as well as his own earlier thoughts.

Some children organize more than one journal or notebook by categories. By the end of his fifth-grade year, Nate had organized his poetry into separate booklets according to nature top-

on after. On piece when
freedom runs in the water
of a stream and fills the
roots of thirsty trees.
Don't fire until you see
the light in your eyes.
Give me liberty or give me
death, 13 clocks striking
as one.
You think you know, but
you don't.
You'll never see yourself
with your eyes closed.
Faded and thin like a
letter read too many times.
When you don't believe in
yourself happiness will be out
of your reach.

A Journey Towards Freedom
By Nate Lohner

The master craftsmanship of that banner filled with red, white, and blue that binds life with freedom.
Every stitch was woven by a history of people who stood for their beliefs.
As thirteen clocks struck as one, a dream was born that dwindled on through fire, smoke, and pain.
The death of multitudes combined as one lives on from sea to sky and spreads through fury, pain, and grief to bring freedom to fly!
We shall take our journey through seas, skies, and land, and take up arms again to fall on golden ground.
A man's first loyalty is for the ground he stands, I must wave a flag so high so all can see it fly.
The blood of our men so free feeds the tree of liberty.
Freedom runs in the water of a stream and fills the roots of thirsty trees.
On this tree that's slowly fed, a fruit grows that feeds the mouths of hungry men.
The sound of guns and mothers' cries if silenced here than freedom dies.
We all shall stand in lines so long and as free men we chose to fall.
Our words all flow from leaders' mouths, give liberty or death.
We waited long till their eyes shone the white that could be seen, that day our freedom flowed.
Through skies and sunset freedom sang with an everlasting shot that echoed through the listeners' ears!
That band of individuals who stood and raised a voice, their crying shrieks are still heard from all who chose to lift an ear.
Through all that's happened liberty still waves that flag so high, it still waves proudly in the wind and shows those who pass by.
Yes we are free with liberty, but debts cannot be paid, to the weavers of that flag who chose this wondrous way.

Figure 8. A comparison of a page of Nate's notebook to an excerpt of a poem he wrote.

ics, family topics, and world peace. Children exhibiting this characteristic of seriously keeping journals should be encouraged to keep and value their journals and notebooks, without being pressured to write in them or share them. These actions can be encouraged by inviting your child to periodically pick out new notebooks, or by giving her several to choose from, while respecting her privacy in what is written in them. My son, who is writing the fantasy trilogy, kept daily entries in several "volumes" of journals at home throughout his second- to fifth-grade years. I didn't even discover this until the summer between his third- and fourth-grade years. I continue to give him new journals each January.

Your child may write more, and more coherently than peers of the same age. It stands to reason that if a child feels an internal compulsion to write, he will do it more often than would be expected of him. He may feel a great sense of confidence in the quality of his writing, and he may find fulfillment in recognizing his own progress. The more he writes, the more he will like what he writes, and the better his writing will become. However, assigned writing practice or rigid expectations for a quota of written pieces will not always have the same effect. The connection between emerging quality to the amount of practice is not a given. Practice can make writing better, but skill and drill will not make thoughtful, gifted writers of our children. Your child's most honest motivation to write comes from within. He will naturally come to seek opportunities to write in order to express ideas or respond to circumstances in which he finds himself. He will enjoy discovering stories, books, or articles to read in comparison to his own writing, or to give him ideas about how to improve some aspect of his writing. He may seek fodder for his imagination in order to create something that is new and exciting. You can support your child's writing interest and ability by pointing out models of print that you enjoy, and sharing in her delight over the writing she produces.

Nate, the fifth grader introduced in Figures 5 and 8, eventually began talking about his writing and himself as a writer in unique ways that were unfamiliar to, and often misunderstood by, the other students in the class. He talked about other authors as if they were his personal acquaintances, and took his writing very seriously as he sought to improve it. Nate often asked his teacher for her opinion or advice about his writing, and earnestly applied her suggestions. This relationship of trust, a sort of mentorship to which Nate responded positively, may not have developed had Emily made numerous assignments for formats and topics of writing. Her writing workshop certainly included instruction in formats and techniques, but it was in response to the needs of her students.

Your child may display a deep desire for the listener or reader to feel something about or because of what has been written. A desire for others to feel strongly about what your child has written may occur simultaneously with her noted preference of taste for a particular genre or author in her reading habits. She may find herself responding or reacting to books or poetry in emotional ways, and striving to communicate similar emotion through her own writing. She may develop a passion for poetry or for letter writing that is more intense than her age- or grade-level peers. She may be keenly interested in researching to write reports on topics of interest to her. If your relationship with your child encourages open discussion of interested or emotional responses to books, movies, poetry, speeches, or other forms of expression, your child will likely share her passionate writing with you, as well. Mem Fox describes growing up in a home where some moments were a "haven of culture and peace." Her father played recordings of classical music while he read and Mem's mother wrote.

What did she write? Letters? Stories? She never told us. But from a young age I noticed her doing it, took in the fact that people wrote for pleasure, and tried it myself from time to time, with satisfying results. (1992, p. 33)

Even beyond feeling peaceful and pleasurable about writing, some young writers may desire to convince their readers that a particular cause is right and true. They may appear to be obsessively concerned about an issue, and display emotional outbursts (positive or negative) while they are thinking and writing on that topic. They may seek feedback from others whom they respect or see as capable of similar emotions. This may be the development of passion in its earliest form. Such passion can be very frustrating to a child when it is not mirrored or validated.

Now that we have discussed some of the characteristics of gifted writers, let's take a look at an extensive range of ways to encourage and empower our writers to open their minds and hearts.

Chapter 2

What Your Child Needs as a Writer

The writer is an explorer. Every stop is an advance into new land.
—*Ralph Waldo Emerson, December 1842*

We all learn to write through reading. We first fall in love with the art of writing when we hear stories and language in books read aloud to us, and then we hear those lovely ideas and that wonderful language even more deeply when we read those books on our own, for ourselves. Through books we learn what makes a good story; what language convinces, persuades, and moves readers; and how good writing sounds. Writing those books, though, is often hard work that takes years of practice, just as any craft or art does. It is important for us to remember that writing, like all life skills, is a lifelong process. Because good writing engages the reader's intelligence and imagination, we can understand that becoming a good writer is a process of continuous engagement in reading and expressing one's own thoughts, as well as the thoughts of others.

I love the title of Ralph Fletcher's book, *What a Writer Needs* (1993), and I am drawn to his ideas for a good portion of what I believe gifted young writers need. Fletcher documents his own journey to his proclamation of self as a writer, and vividly illustrates the support he drew upon to get there. The ideas of others such as Lucy Calkins (2000), Caryn Mirriam-Goldberg (1999), Katie Wood Ray (1999, 2002), Georgia Heard (1995), and Ronald L. Cramer (2001) have also influenced my passion about gifted young writers. After my own classroom observations and discussions with parents and teachers of young writers, I have expanded, trimmed, grafted, and groomed my own list of what gifted young writers need. This list includes some general ideas about child-appropriate intellectual freedoms that are critical to the necessary sense of freedom we wish our young writers to develop (see Table 3).

Some of these supports are needed by all writers, but I hope to convince you that gifted young writers need these elements in unique ways or in more quantity than the average beginning writer. All children deserve them, but gifted writers *need* them. If you believe in the emotional and philosophical support these ideas offer for your child, the actual tasks, strategies, and activities in which you and your child engage will be much more effective and provide lasting results.

What Writers Need

First, writers need *immersion* in a print-rich environment. Marie-Henri Beyle was an 18th-century novelist who wrote under the pseudonym Stendhal. The Stendhal Effect is attributed

---

Table 3
What Writers Need

Writers need:
- immersion in a print-rich environment,
- adaptations for more effective learning,
- mentors,
- powerful teachers,
- aspirations for high standards of quality,
- validation of their strengths and a thrust beyond them,
- their originality and diversity valued,
- encouragement to take risks,
- routines that inspire predictable security, and
- permission for their passion.

---

to him because he wrote of how beauty has the power to stun people—to stir their emotional and physical responses. Children need a stimulating, accepting environment full of books, posters, fine art, and opportunities to share these inspirations with significant adults and peers in their lives. They deserve to witness how the Stendhal Effect influences others, and recognize when they are affected by it, as well. If the environment in our homes is not already rich in print materials, we can transform it in ways that will uplift, give energy, and excite a passion for reading and writing. There are multiple resources to help you fill your home with print materials in Chapter 5, but the most meaningful environment will be one wherein your and your child's personalities are evident—where new books are savored as delightful treats or rare works of art or where writer's notebooks are kept by both the parent and child. Our goal should be to create a home that invites our children in and makes them want to be there and enjoy thinking, feeling, and learning with us in this place.

Next, writers need *adaptations* of our focus on their learning. By this I mean that the frameworks for discussion of literacy in the home can be adapted or adjusted to meet the unique and specific needs of the child. For example, entire celebrations of birthdays or holidays can be organized around important themes our children find interesting in

> Our goal should be to create a home that invites our children in and makes them want to be there and enjoy thinking, feeling, and learning with us in this place.

literature. For instance, in the days leading up to her birthday, a very young child who loves stuffed animals could be exposed to famous teddy bear literature, such as A. A. Milne's *Winnie the Pooh,* and she could investigate nonfiction literature for the origination of teddy bears. As a culmination, this teddy bear lover and new authority on the subject could be taken to a retail establishment where the bear is actually constructed as the child watches and makes choices for each part of the bear's construction.

An older child could be introduced to literature about baseball, including multiple published versions of *Casey at the Bat* by Ernest Lawrence Thayer, as well as *The Greatest Baseball Stories Ever Told*, edited by Jeff Silverman. After investigating every genre's application of a baseball theme, a culminating event might not only include tickets to a baseball game, but a visit to the area where the sports journalists convene and work, and a subsequent reading of every print review that can be found concerning that game.

Did you know that every culture in the known world has its own version of a Cinderella tale? Start with a search at the library or bookstore for all of the versions you can find of the familiar story. Then do an Internet search for published versions from other countries, cultures, and ethnic groups. Find as many as you can and compare them. Find what they have in common and how

| **Table 4** |
| **Who Are Good Writing Mentors?** |
| Parents |
| Teachers |
| College students |
| College professors |
| Poets-in-residence |
| Newspaper reporters |
| Librarians |
| Magazine editors/publishers |
| Book editors/publishers |

they differ. Determine what makes them unique to their origination. Vote on your favorites. Retell them to others. Speak with college professors of children's literature or folk literature. Tour European castles in person or on film. High school girls might enjoy a study of "And Then the Prince Knelt Down and Tried to Put the Glass Slipper on Cinderella's Foot," by Judith Viorst, a story in *Don't Bet on the Prince: Contemporary Feminist Fairy Tales in North America and England* by Jack Zipes, published in 1987. Possibilities for themed investigation ideas are endless, and literature searches are easier than ever because of Internet search engines.

Writers need *mentors*—wise and caring people who know them and have hope for their potential. A child who loves to write deserves a mentor who has an intuitive sense for his delicate curiosity, his hopes, talents, and dreams, as well as a realistic view of his frustrations, misconceptions, and limitations. Young writers need mentors who know something about the craft of writing. Table 4 presents a list of people who often make good writing mentors.

There are classrooms and teachers aplenty who reduce writing instruction to a simplistic system of exercises and assignments. Gifted writers need to see writing beyond the assignment. Talented writers deserve to concentrate on the *craft* of writing as a developmental and dynamic growth process toward a sophisticated proficiency. This process can only be shared by teachers, parents, or mentors who have a deep and profound knowledge and appreciation for the craft of writing. This does not mean that the teachers of young writers must be *gifted* writers themselves; teachers do well when they have at least felt, even minimally, the writing process from the inside out. But, it does mean that the teachers must have immersed themselves in good writing, availed themselves of the elements of good writing, and have acquainted themselves with the authors and creators of the best in writing.

Young writers need mentors who, rather than present themselves as masters of written communication, model the very struggles and processes they hope to see in the child's writing. Young writers do not need strict taskmasters standing over their writing with red pen in hand, nor praise for every word that they put to paper or computer screen. Young writers *do* need mentors who will sit alongside them and collaboratively struggle through the process and share the glory of the written word. The best mentors know when to give all they know, when to withhold all they can give, and when to watch, judge, and help "with the wisdom of a good gardener" (Arnheim, 1989, p. 37). Good mentors will strive to unlock the child's creative potential; they understand that the child's mind and spirit are as fragile as they are malleable. Ronald Cramer (2001) has said, "Children are artists of language, not language scholars. They use language not to impress but to express. Given a little fall of rain from a fine teacher, children can make the flowers grow" (p. xiv).

I tend to side with Mem Fox (1993), again, who believes it helps if teachers of writing "have been soldiers themselves, engaged in a writing battle," because they can "empathize more closely with the comrades in their classrooms than teachers who are merely war correspondents . . . watching the battle from a safe distance" (p. 11).

Next, writers need *powerful teachers*. Mem Fox (1993) said, "I wish we could change the world by creating powerful writers for forever instead of just indifferent writers for school" (p. 22). We can! Powerful teachers can. Consider the term *teacher* as referring to you in that role, or find someone who can function in this role. Children are drawn to teachers who possess a creative and artistic spirit, either in what they, the teachers, are capable of, or in their ability to observe and recognize creativity and artistic vision in others. Writing teachers should take part in the creative process their students are engaged in. As Donald Murray (2003) says, "Teachers should write so they understand the process of writing from within" (p. 74). Powerful teachers can share their passion in personal stories of their own and others' creative efforts, struggles, and persistence. Powerful teachers motivate children through carefully guided choice and experimentation, not unrestricted options. Writing instruction is more than teaching the rules and procedures of standard communication. It is more a process of teaching critical thinking, as well as helping young writers to know and understand themselves and others.

Powerful teachers require young writers to examine and explore the world around them, to look closely at their relationships, and to expand their senses of perspective and personal relevance. Powerful teachers prepare their students for lives beyond the home and classroom. Powerful teachers instill the ability to both construct meaning and to share meaning with others in clear, concise, and compelling ways. They recognize that it is only through effectual interaction with ideas that the child will grow as a writer. However you get to the vision, passion, and motivation of a powerful teacher, gifted writers deserve whatever it takes.

Young writers need aspiration to *high standards of quality*. In order to develop a sense of quality writing to which they should aspire, children must be exposed to a variety of types, genres, styles, and authors. Children deserve to have favorites, and to study and pursue their favorites with breadth and depth. They can benefit from learning about the specific characteristics and techniques they observe and discover in quality writing. How can they distinguish quality writing? By your sharing and discussing how passages, endings, or whole stories make you feel. What's so funny about that comic strip? What moves you in that essay? Additionally, you can help teach your child about quality when you share reviews of books you or your child have read.

Children can come to understand literary criticism at some level, and to develop goals for the quality of their own writing when the process of analyzing literature is an enjoyable experience from which memorable moments grow. Authentic connections between good literature and your child's desires to write occur when she understands your emotional responses and opinions and perceives that you are affirming hers.

In fact, when it comes right down to it, once we get beyond the physical act of forming letters into words on paper, writing is a lot about caring what other people think about what *we think*. Children can write well when they care about what they are writing, and desire for their readers to care about it also. This is the key to helping our children be influenced by high standards—to care about reaching the standards. Mem Fox (1993) observed that nearly all of her writing had "the socially interactive purpose of either creating relationships or ensuring that established relationships continue" (p. 9). While she is writing, she thinks of someone who will be reading her words as

> . . . invisibly watching me write, waiting to read what I've written. . . . The more I admire my potential readers, the more carefully I write and the more often I revise. . . . How often are our students able to receive a response from someone they particularly admire? . . . I think we tend to forget about this element of relationships when we teach writing. . . . Do we remember how much the caring over their writing is often also an aching to make friends with us and with their peers? (Fox, 1993, p. 9–11)

Children need and will aspire to high standards of quality in their writing when their desire to create and affect relationships through what they write is validated, encouraged, and facilitated.

Young writers need *validation of their strengths and a thrust beyond them*. One aspect of validation is meaningful response from others who are affected by their writing. As Mem Fox (1993) says, "Children develop language through interaction, not action. They learn to talk by talking to someone who responds. They must therefore learn to write by writing to someone who responds" (p. 22).

When response is sincere, specific, and indicative of understanding what the writer has intended, the writer approaches a position of acceptance and strength from which she can forge ahead to the hard work of progress and improvement. Validation does not mean a loss of individuality toward a common judgment, but a value for what is individually and inherently distinguished. It does not mean a glossing over of problems or weaknesses, but rather an admired sense of differentiating between what is splendid and what can be enhanced. Validation does not include requiring a child to adhere to set structures of writing that push them to change their ideas in order to fill in the blanks, but rather, an accepting and understanding of their desires and ability to express their thoughts and emotions with words. The key to validation that pushes the young writer to the next stage or stepping stone is specificity.

"Writers tend to be fragile, highly sensitive, breakable creatures," say Ralph Fletcher and JoAnn Portalupi (2001, p. 51). "Student writers aren't always open to suggestions, from us or from their peers. That's why it's so important to give them concrete praise," even for small or isolated elements of their writing. Pointing out weaknesses may be palatable to your child if you often focus on her strengths, and if the direction is specific. In pointing out her weaknesses, present them one at a time as an exciting problem to solve, a fun puzzle to figure out, or a challenge to uniqueness. Then find solutions together in an uplifting manner where you both learn and grow.

Writers need their *diversity and originality valued*. Writing is a vehicle for your child to discover what he knows about himself and the world. American poet William Stafford once said that a writer is not someone who has something to say as much as someone who has *found* a way to say it. Writing allows your child to explore what he loves and hates, what he needs and can give, and what he wants from the world. The very act of writing—making something out of nothing—produces a feeling of worth and sense of accomplishment. This helps your child believe in himself and increase his self-efficacy. Perhaps most importantly, writing allows your child to hear her own unique voice,

> Writing allows your child to explore what he loves and hates, what he needs and can give, and what he wants from the world.

to communicate in her own words, and to be herself. Your recognition of and affirmative response to your child's unique voice will help her to recognize it and to know herself better. When we honor the uniqueness of each child, we are able to show profound respect for what each has to say, which in turn, encourages your child to continue revealing himself to us through his words. Empowering a child's unique voice is about encouraging her to communicate her personal truth—her thoughts, feelings, ideas, and emotions—in writing. "Where truth thrives, individuality also flourishes" (Spandel, 2005a, p. 140).

Emerging writers need to *take risks*, and they benefit from strong and caring encouragement to do so. Writing is a safe way to test the waters with questions and beliefs, seek answers and feedback, and to observe what happens because of creative ideas. Creation of anything requires us to ask questions, dwell at least momentarily in doubt and confusion, and to finally reach a breakthrough. As your child writes, he will immerse himself in the creative process, and the more practice he has in this, the more easily he will be able to transfer these skills to other areas of his life that require creative solutions. He needs your support and concern, with healthy amounts of freedom, in order to do so. He will benefit from your pointing out risks that are apparent to you as you discover new authors or new books that intrigue you. This will model to your child safety in having and sharing opinions, and the value you place on uniqueness and creative endeavors.

"Without risk, it is nearly impossible to grow as a writer" (Spandel, 2005a, p. 63). Sure, non-risk-takers can rise to a level of competence and produce prolific products that contain all the necessary data and most of the conventions. But, is that enough? Is that all we want for them, when they could do so much more? Truly gifted communication is "unlikely to happen, though, if we insist that they write well or even adequately *all the time*. No one does this. No one who writes to be read, anyway" (Spandel, 2005a, p. 63). Author Stephen King has said, "Only God gets it right the first time" (2000, p. 212).

Many young writers need *routines that inspire predictable security*. Apply routines with discrimination and with great care to support risk-taking, rather than discourage it. Routines can be as simple as having a family "word of the day," or tuning in to a radio program such as "All Things Considered" on National Public Radio. For many people, routines provide the best way to diet, to get in physical shape, or to learn a skill such as playing tennis. The same principles of predictable sequences or repetitions of activities can be helpful in developing the writing craft. However, dieting can become a straightjacket for someone with an eating disorder, and tennis elbow can result from repetitive and vigorous use or overuse of the forearm muscles. Introducing routines one at a time in a lighthearted manner can enhance the effect they have on your child's desire to engage in them. Routines in which your child assumes the role of researcher or presenter can inspire him to enjoy the habit and use it to energize himself for writing tasks. The following routines may be fun to initiate with your child:

- *Experts:* You and/or your child find fascinating facts to share about a writer, her history, or how she approaches writing a new book, poem, or article.
- *Riddle of the day:* Riddles have potential to trigger critical thinking and problem solving, and allow you to enjoy words and imaginative language.
- *Word of the day:* This involves you or your child choosing a word (e.g., critique, montage, onomatopoeia, metamorphosis, or many others) and displaying it prominently. Effective vocabulary teaching involves saying the word, using it in con-

text, explaining or showing examples, and then challenging each other to think of sentences using the word.

- *A poem a day:* This routine can begin with displaying or just reading a poem. The poem is read expressively so that the sounds and images can be enjoyed. The family can choral-read it, whisper read it, act it out, or just add it to a family collection. Jacqueline Kennedy had her children select or write poems as gifts to their father, President John F. Kennedy, for every birthday and holiday. This routine instilled a lifelong love for poetry in their daughter, Caroline, who recently published two collections of family favorites (*A Family of Poems: My Favorite Poetry for Children*, 2005, and *The Best Loved Poems of Jacqueline Kennedy-Onassis*, 2001).

- *Words for life journals:* By using a journal routine that focuses on observations, descriptions, and lists, you and your child can discover how much all published books, poetry, and articles are influenced by what the writer documents. A variety of little books for the very purpose of taking notes on reading are available for purchase at bookstores. Three of my favorites:
  - *Books to Check Out: A Journal*, published in 2001 by Chronicle Books
  - *Reading Notes*, published in 2005 by Ryland, Peters & Small
  - *Book Club Journal: A Workbook and Record Keeper*, published in 2003 by Peter Pauper Press, Inc.

Young gifted writers need *permission for their passion* for writing. Because writing forces your child to sit and think, it can be a way for him to find answers to questions that arise in his life. Writing is introspective by nature, and gives the writer opportunities to carefully review choices and decisions, to examine his questions, and to find answers that fit in his world, which you have helped create. Writing will help your child to reveal aspects of himself that don't always come across in face-to-face communication, phone conversations, class presentations, or family discussions. As a writer, your child will have more time to reflect on what he believes, what he wants to say, and why he thinks or feels a certain way. Writers all eventually need to feel empowered to make a difference with their writing. Giving young writers permission for their passion for writing is, I believe, the most important ingredient to give writers, along with mentors, high standards, appreciation for their ideas and uniqueness, and the feeling of security when they take risks. It may help to ask ourselves when we or our children last ached with passion over what we were writing, or wrote, because it mattered deeply. When have you written because you have had a huge investment in your writing?

It is not likely that you picked up this book out of an obligation to become a writer yourself. Then again, the title peaked your curiosity in some way—you were drawn to the idea of your child's writing, because of the passion you have already observed emanating from your child, or there is a seed of passion in you, either lying dormant, or attempting to germinate. The ideas about writing in this book also should appeal to you, in either regard. These ideas are wonderful and true, based in the real world of writers at work.

> [These writing ideas] will fail only if we . . . refuse to write ourselves, to learn firsthand the fear of rejection; the fear of self-exposure; the horror of writing; the pleasure of having an appreciative audience; and the necessity for a reason, a reader, and a real reaction. We ourselves must write in order to spread the word with conviction. (Fox, 1993, p. 40)

Conviction is closely related to passion. When we provide a consistent diet of this conviction—permission for passion—in a long-term environment of support and validation, we empower our children to see themselves as the writers they are becoming.

Treat Writing as Thinking

Writing allows the writer time to think again, and to choose thoughts and words carefully. Writers don't usually "know beforehand where to begin, much less how to proceed" (Nagin & National Writing Project, 2003, p. 9). Writing gives the writer access to strategies that can lift the quality of thinking to a limitless potential for pondering, observing, cutting, extending, leaving behind and returning to thoughts, and many other steps that make the writing just right. In fact, the more complex the subject is, the more disorganized and unpredictable the act of composing what the writer wants to say is. Therefore, writing can create deeper thinking than other means of communication allow. Writing is hard work because "it is a struggle of thought, feeling, and imagination to find expression clear enough for the task at hand (Nagin & National Writing Project, p. 9). Ronald Cramer (2001) has established five characteristics of writing that influence thinking, found in Table 5.

Make a Mark, Leave a Record, Tell a Story

I take enormous pleasure every time I see something that I've done that cannot be wiped out. In some way . . . I guess it's a protest against mortality. But it's been so much fun! . . . It's making a difference in the world that prevents me from ever giving up.

—Deborah Meier, educator, 1992

**Table 5
Five Characteristics of Writing That
Influence Thinking**

1. Writing is visible: E. M. Forster said, "How can I know what I think until I see what I say?" Sartre, the French existentialist, is said to have quit writing when his eyesight deteriorated because he could no longer see the words. Apparently, Sartre, like most writers, needed to manipulate the visible symbols of thought in order to generate the meaning he wished to convey. No longer able to visualize his thoughts, Sartre found writing impossible. Writing makes visible what is ordinarily invisible—thought. Once thought is made visible through written symbols, it can be manipulated. The visibility of written thought enables writers to discover relationships among ideas they might have missed if thought depended entirely on verbal manipulations.

2. Writing is permanent: Oral language is forgettable, a funeral. Once words are spoken they cannot be recaptured or even remembered for very long. Not so with writing. Writing leaps the bonds of time and space, and gives eternal life to our words and ideas. Writing is the repository of humanity's accumulated knowledge.

3. Writing is active: Writing is active, a search for meaning enlisting the resources of mind and body. Writing involves the physical task of depicting writing: handwriting, spelling, punctuation, depressing the keys on the typewriter or computer, erasing, crossing out, rereading, rewriting.

4. Writing is precise: Writing disciplines the mind into precise formulation of its thoughts. This is what Francis Bacon had in mind when he said, "Reading maketh a full man, conference a ready man, and writing an exact man" (Ehrlich & DeBruhl, 1996, p. 766). Of course, written language is not inherently precise. Like oral language, it is subject to the vagaries of the sender and the receiver. Nevertheless, as a form of communication, writing holds the greater promise of precision.

Table 5, continued
5. Writing focuses thinking: Few activities focus the mind as keenly as writing. Revision is especially effective in refocusing thinking, since it enables us to rethink our first draft thoughts. Writing enables us to summon thoughts out of darkness and into the light.
Note. From *Creative Power: The Nurture and Nature of Children's Writing* (p. 3), by R. L. Cramer, 2001, Allyn & Bacon, Boston. Copyright ©2001 by Pearson Education. Reprinted with permission of the publisher.

Families *should* be writing—recollections, whims, stories of love and pain, laughter and lessons, troubling, sad, or silly things—all of the rich stuff that makes a family the unique legacy it is. A child who grows up in a family that enjoys writing cannot help but come to value writing. Whether or not she becomes a professional writer, her skills, perceptions, and even her test scores, will be enhanced and increased because she has been a vital part of a writing family. She will have interacted with words that have gone straight to her heart, and with the writers of those words whom she cares the most about. There may not be a greater or wiser gift than that of words written down.

Look around your home. Where do you find signs of a writing family? Are there current journals being kept by family members, or journals passed down from a previous generation to yours? Are letters written, received, and saved? Are there any closet poets among you—who turn every invitation or funny memory into a simple rhyme? Has anyone captured your funniest stories or most priceless, touching memories? Could a snoopy visitor to your home find any supply of paper and pens or pencils? If you do nothing else to encourage your

> There may not be a greater or wiser gift than that of words written down.

child as a serious writer, you will be doing a favor for your family now and in future generations if you will choose a starting place and begin your family's writing life. Here are some ideas to get you started:

- *When I was your age . . .* What if never a birthday or holiday went by without your child receiving a written form of a memory from you when you were 6, 8, or 16 years of age? These could be collected in a treasured notebook, pages added to an empty journal, or framed.

- *We won't remember it if we don't write it down.* What funny phrase did your 3-year-old utter today? What funny or touching, never-to-be-repeated observation have you jotted down today, this week? One thing is for sure: You won't remember it if you don't write it down.

- *Twenty-five wonderful words.* As a family, compile an ongoing list of 25 words that family members like—any words. Encourage all family members to contribute. Keep them posted in a place where the family gathers fairly regularly (near the kitchen table or in the family room). Talk about them, play guessing games with them, or form riddles about them ("Guess which word I'm thinking of . . . "). Hold holiday word campaigns, where family members promote words in an election or contest, using posters, banners, slogans, buttons, and even speeches to convince others to vote for their word. Visit grandparents or neighbors to ask for their votes.

- *Scrapbooking current and family events.* Keep a family scrapbook and take turns describing events and illustrating them with sketches, photos, or cut-outs and clip art. This scrapbook can be in the form of a simple three-ring, loose-leaf notebook, or a commercially prepared scrapbook with big, wide pages that invite the addition of information.

- *Family word collages.* Each family member can create a self-describing word collage with cut-out words from magazines, junk mail, and other disposable print. For an anniversary (the family's "birthday," or the "birthday" of some important direction your family has taken), create a family celebration word collage.
- *Family e-mail editors.* Rotate through your family members an e-mail editor who is responsible for notifying family members of the types of e-mail that have come, and summarizing what the mail is. Your child will experience examples of e-mail etiquette and skills related to composing e-mail. If he does not already have access to writing e-mail, this would be a great introduction to his being able to participate safely in this world of cyber communication.
- *Whys and why nots.* Have you ever drawn a line down the middle of a sheet of paper, and written the pros and cons of a problem to solve or a decision to be made? Writing fosters vision, although too many people only believe the reverse of that sentence. If you write when you are baffled, angry, or depressed, something is sure to rise to the surface.
- *Lists, lists, and more lists.* Days after one of my friends passed away, too early and unexpectedly, her teenage daughters found interesting lists in the drawer of her nightstand. One list included 10 dates, which the girls determined to be the 10 most important dates in their mother's life ... days like meeting their dad, marrying him, each of the girls' birthdates, and the date of the one Mother's Day where the girls really did shower their mother with love, favors, breakfast in bed, and entertainment. Think of what lists can reveal about you: lists of favorite words, lists of people you've always disliked and why (with notes about your feelings that may have changed over time), lists of five decisions you've been putting off, a

list of five or six people to whom you should write, thanking them for their influence, lists of lifelong frustrations, and lists of items and events that bring you joy.

- *Closet graffiti.* Use the inside of a closet door that only the family will see. Attach a large sheet of poster paper or freezer paper to the inside door, and place some colored markers close to the paper. Allow doodlings and wonderings to be placed on the paper. Family members can contribute when something is on their minds, or when they have a question to which they don't need a serious response. The only requirement to join in the fun is to be able to convey meaning with a comment, question, or drawing. The more your additions resemble graffiti, the more interesting your closet becomes.

- *Journals and journaling.* The simplest and, perhaps purest, form of writing may be the observable act of making an entry in a journal. It is a private act, accomplished for and by yourself, but typically an unselfish conscious act. It amounts to a congenial transaction between you and an empty page in an empty or half-filled book. There are no rules, no expectations, and no compelling reason to keep writing in a journal, except for insights you may recognize at a later time when you really need it, or personal revelations to an adult child or grandchild about yourself after you are gone. The physical book in which you keep your journal can be almost as motivating as the thoughts and events you wish to describe in it.

- *Love note mania.* Write and share with each other tributes, odes, love songs, or love notes to unusual items, such as your nose, lightning, December, a math test, your soccer ball, dirty socks, or dust on the furniture.

- *People watching.* Keep a people watching notebook in the car, and take it along on vacations, dinner outings, or leisurely Sunday afternoon drives. Rotate turns through family members to record observations of one or more persons you can watch for at least a few minutes, or have each family member write a description of a different person in the setting you are in. Try it once, or create a traveling tradition. You will be surprised at how your stories will become part of your family lore, and make their way into your child's writer's notebook, poems, or stories.

- *Letters.* It can be fascinating to read collections of letters from others through the ages, whether they are from Civil War soldiers, Beethoven, Charles Lindbergh to Anne Marrow, or from Anne to Charles. So, write some letters, and whether or not you send them, keep copies of them for some other day and time.

- *Postcards from yourself to yourself.* As you travel, have your child write on postcards and send them home to himself. Adding to his own collection of memories and pictures from his travels can motivate him to experiment with descriptive writing and mimicking travel brochures and tour guides.

- *Things I wish I could do.* I don't know if Jerry Spinelli wrote his list of 16 things he wished he could do when he was 16 years old, or about being 16, or if he simply chose a random number of items to place on his list. I love this list! It includes trivial pursuits such as the ability to "spit between my two front teeth" to breaking a popsicle perfectly down the middle to have two equal parts, all the way to his more contemplative desires such as to "understand eternity" (Spinelli, 1998, p. 76). The list reveals volumes about Spinelli's personality, his hopes and dreams, his sense of humor, and some of his childhood and adolescent beliefs. Spinelli's list has inspired me to have my children write a new list each year. When my daughter turns 18 this year, I will be very interested in what her list says about what she wishes she could do. I wish I had a list of eight things from when she was 8 years old, nine things she wished she could do at age 9, and so on. What a wonderful record I would have if I had compiled lists from each year of my child's life—a delightful little sample of her growing and changing values, hopes, and dreams.

- *Word of the day.* Responsibility for choosing a new word and presenting it in a delightful way can rotate through the family. Other word games, rhyming games, and Mad Libs can be found in books and on Web sites, and can inspire fun for family members in spare moments between meals or other home activities.

- *Words as gifts.* Start a tradition and give your words away. Write messages to your child when you are away; write your memories of your parents' marriage for their anniversary; create a memory book or collection of words that many people have written; give words back—words that you remember the recipient has said to you, entitled "Words of Wisdom," "Words of Wit," or "Words of Love."

- *Family recipe book.* Great as gifts to extended family and your own children, these can be fascinating records of not only what generations of your family has eaten, but who thought what about the food, or interesting sources of beloved good meals. The way you write up the recipes and descriptions can bring to mind aromas, textures, and tastes from your and others' childhoods.

- *Poetry magnets.* Inexpensive sets of small magnetic word strips are available at bookstores and through mail order catalogs. They are also easy to make from printing words that are found in a variety of poems, adhering the page to thin magnetic sheets, and cutting the words apart. It makes it fun to leave poetic messages to each other on the refrigerator.

- *Golden book lines.* Encourage your child to find golden lines as they are reading—sentences that especially attract them and inspire them to notice clever or colorful writing. Find a golden foil-covered journal for writing down these golden lines to share and reread later.
- *Family newsletters.* Folks who have been writing and sending these for years might not think there's anything special about them. But, if you are in the habit of sending a family newsletter out, you will have a vehicle with which to entice your budding author—your child as a writer. Your child may become a feature writer, or even the editor in chief.

Can you see how the simplest endeavor and a little bit of time can provide the visibility, permanence, preciseness, sincerity, and focus of thought that can enhance your child's life as a writer? In fact, families writing together can enhance the essence of your lives altogether. The benefits are far reaching, and you may come to find that you enjoy the responsibility and opportunity of enhancing and inspiring the thinking and writing in your home. So, how much responsibility should your child's school assume? In the next chapter we will investigate the parent-teacher partnerships that affect our children as writers.

Working With the School to Encourage Your Child as a Writer

I will create a class culture of questioning. . . . If I have 120 students, I will have 120 teacher's aides. I will train students to assess and reflect on their own work daily and take charge of their learning.
—*Barry Lane, 1999*

A teacher's job is to teach children not only to write, but also to want to write. Really, what we call *language arts* in the school curriculum centers around the ability to communicate effectively, including a critical focus on writing. Throughout a child's life, standardized assessments of his ability to communicate will occur largely through determining his ability to write. However, it is increasingly more difficult to carve out adequate time for teaching writing in today's regular elementary and middle school classrooms. Teachers are justifiably asking, "How do I find the time to focus on these students as individual writers with so much else to cover?" You may discover that where there is a personal commitment to writing as an expressive, thinking process from a teacher or grade-level team of teachers, the dynamic teaching of writing is happening. If this is the situation in which you and your child find yourselves, congratulations! Your work will be often supplementary in nature, and you will feel like a member of a team.

Whether your child is in a public or private school, or a regular classroom or some type of advanced placement situation, if it is evident that the authentic, meaningful writing process is not a priority in the classroom, you face a dilemma. Will the situation improve with hard work or a moderate amount of mediation on your part, or will it be a matter of your being willing to endure with your child a few months of no progress at school while you focus your energies on what you can do for your child on your own? If you choose to work with the school, you *can* find ways to assist the school in providing what your child needs as a writer. It won't be simple, and there is no guarantee that you will bring about permanent positive change.

How can you help? First, as simplistic as it sounds, it is an absolute foundation for taking on the task of affecting change: Know yourself and know your child, know good literature that will inspire young writers, know a handful of the best teaching methods, and know what a gifted writer needs. It should sound familiar, for these are the same foundational attitudes required to help your child's writing ability at home. Armed with this knowledge of self, your child, inspiring literature, a few effective teaching methods, and the needs of gifted writers—you can endeavor to support and even advance the ability of your child's teacher to provide for your child's writing needs.

> Know yourself and know your child, know good literature that will inspire young writers, know a handful of the best teaching methods, and know what a gifted writer needs.

Introducing Your Writer to the School

While it may seem that teachers should desire and be able to discover and nurture their students' writing ability, you may find it necessary to illuminate the issue of your child's ability, talent, or passion in this area, and to inspire or promote the teacher's support of it. Generally speaking, teachers have been circumstantially conditioned to look at the class as a whole and to apply their knowledge and skills toward educating the class in general. Your advocacy for your child can be problematic when a teacher perceives that you know more or *think* you know more than he or she does. Education has a long history of turf wars when it comes to decisions about what and how things should be taught.

Your child's teacher may not recognize your child's potential or abilities as a writer. He or she may not be looking for exceptional ability or passion for writing because national and state mandates and standards place additional stresses on teachers' planning. These stresses continue to rise year after year, clouding and often blocking the teachers' ability to persistently teach for the children's truest lifelong advantage. In any group of public educators, you will quickly and clearly hear complaints about outside or additional expectations they feel may hinder their attempts to save the struggling readers in their classrooms, or prevent them from efficiently covering the curriculum they are required to teach. On the other hand, some teachers simply do not understand what it means to discover the communicator in each child, nor to empower students to express their true selves through writing.

Positive Ways to Work With the School

There is much that parents can do, and it all begins with developing some form of mutual trust with the teacher. This should be the driving force in all parent-teacher interactions. After all, you and the teacher share this child for several hours of the day, for several weeks of the year.

Find Something in Common

Look for common ground in philosophy in order to appeal to the teacher's desires to nurture growth and opportunity for each of her students. When the teacher discusses philosophy or explains procedures at parent night, follow up with a positive-toned letter or a well-timed verbal response that compliments what you heard and how it corresponds with what you believe about your child. This kind of initial communication cannot be stressed enough, for it allows the teacher to hear and remember what you say, and to see you not only as an involved parent, but also as an ally to the teacher. When letters come home from the school with explanations of classroom activities or invitations for volunteers, find some way to respond with the greatest amount and quality of support and assistance that you can give. Of course, this is an opportunity to enhance your child's experience. But, you should recognize it, as well, as an opportunity for the teacher to become acquainted with you and appreciate your interest in enhancing the experience for all of his students, as well as for your own child.

Volunteer Your Time

Volunteer to help the teacher initiate something he has wanted to do with writing in the classroom, to carry out a new schoolwide mandate about which he is reluctant, or to maintain a program that he has already begun. An acquaintance of mine has made it a habit to volunteer to facilitate special writing contests or programs in her child's classroom. When my friend's daughter was a fifth-grade student, this child was miserable during the several hours of spelling and grammar workbook exercises, and reading and answering low-level questions at the ends of basal reading chapters. My friend researched and learned about several creative writing contest options that allowed for differentiated writing projects according to areas of interest and ability. She met with the teacher and presented these as projects that she, the parent, would be willing to assist in if the teacher wished. The teacher had heard about one of the contests, and jumped at the chance to involve her students. With the help of a knowledgeable and capable parent as a partner, the teacher was able to provide enhancing opportunities for her students. The key to this successful situation was the homework done by the parent to find options that fit with what she knew about the teacher and the curriculum, and then the kind and unobtrusive, but specifically appropriate, way she volunteered to help.

Research Opportunities and Options

Suggest a variety of options for special classroom programs or activities that appeal to the teacher because they support his ideas or desires, appear to be low maintenance in labor and cost, and integrate other content areas with which he is concerned. This, again, will take some research on your part, but the benefits of what can be provided for your child can far outweigh your investment of time. Perhaps you can find local or national writing contests (see resources provided in Chapter 5) and present them in ways that illustrate to the teacher the benefits of becoming involved. Partnering with the teacher in implementation or assisting him as the leader in the project can prevent power struggles and can enhance the experience for all students in the classroom, thus making your child's encounter even better.

Compliment the Teacher for Following the Standards

Praise your child's teacher for how his or her classroom advances the state or national writing standards, even if you can find only a small amount of compliance. Of course, first you will need to know about the standards. All state and national standards involved with literacy and writing instruct that children write daily, including those from the National Council of Teachers of English, which can be obtained from its Web site, http://www. ncte.org. You also may feel comfortable in sharing printed information, such as the pamphlet, *30 Ideas for Teaching Writing,* free from the National Writing Project (visit http://www.writingproject.org or call the national office at 510-642-0963 to receive a copy of this pamphlet). The teacher should recognize either the NCTE standards or the National Writing Project, and if you base your compliments to the teacher on what you have learned from their materials, your credibility should be affirming. Be sure to use materials authored by credible and respected organizations and researchers that will stand a good chance of being recognized in the school system, and not discounted as unqualified information.

As a parent of a writer, you can feel confident and reassured about your child's teacher if he or she views students as writers from the very first day of school, whether they are in ninth grade

> As a parent of a writer, you can feel confident and reassured about your child's teacher if he or she views students as writers from the very first day of school.

or kindergarten. You should be pleased if traditional workbooks have been replaced with personal journals and child-authored booklets or other publications, produced by both individual children and the whole class. In this kind of classroom environment, spelling and grammar instruction are approached as tools that enable writers to be authors. Spelling and writing errors are recognized as a necessary and acceptable part of learning to use the language and successfully communicate.

Some confusion is understandable if the instruction your child experiences differs dramatically from what you received in school. Parents often ask, "What was wrong with the way I learned? I loved workbooks, language tests, and spelling bees!" Take it upon yourself to learn and understand the rationale behind many of today's less didactic and less autocratic methods of instruction that are personally validating and developmentally tuned to the right knowledge and instruction at the right time. Some of the old drill and practice time has given way to time for inspiration, discussion, and sharing. A former student of mine, Natalie, who is now a second-grade teacher in a year-round school, recently told me that her class had just come back from being off track for 2 weeks.

> When I announced on Thursday that we would be doing writers' workshop, my students cheered! It was the best noise ever—cheering for writing time! They love it. I really do know the importance of the first step: inspire. During my inspiration time, my students all have little handheld notebooks. They write their ideas in their notebooks, whenever one pops into their heads. Sometimes I wonder if they even listen to my inspiration story because they are all writing down ideas. Then when I ask for volunteers to share their writing, they all want to share. Even the shy ones! (N. Spencer, personal communication, September 11, 2005)

Natalie shared the following conversation she overheard between a new student who had moved into the class and the "buddy" Natalie had assigned to him.

Buddy:	Now is the time when you write about one of the ideas in your idea book.
New Student:	I want to write about food.
Buddy:	You can write about anything you want.
New Student:	Can I make it into a poem?
Buddy:	Yeah, you can write whatever you want.
New Student:	This is so cool!

While instruction and practice of spelling and grammar skills are critical to the development of communication ability, it is helpful for you to recognize that heavy emphasis on correct spelling and grammar (especially in the *idea* and *drafting* stages for young children, and the *idea* stage for older students) can encourage debilitating perfectionism and induce a fear of taking the risk to write. Most misspellings, grammatical errors, and other unconventional aspects of writing will be outgrown, and can actually become strengths if they are handled with the proper perspective through the years of your child's maturing and development.

It is more important for your child to express original ideas and get them onto paper than to spell correctly. This is, unequivocally, the truth for the initial stages in the writing process, but let me qualify it. Your support of a teacher who works with this more open-ended, empowering mode of writing instruction can help to create marvelous strides in your child's writing development. Children who learn to write in these circumstances enjoy writing, and seek to improve their writing out of an innate sense of standards and motivation, rather than to earn a grade. Their understanding and skills in spelling and writing conventions will increase and improve out of their desire to refine and perfect their communication, the writing they have come to know powerfully as their own.

Writing Clubs

Some schools have initiated writing clubs that meet during the noon hour or after school. These clubs typically are supervised by a faculty member or parent. Your child may enjoy an opportunity to participate in a writing club, or to form one if none already exist. If you child is in elementary school, you may be able to initiate a before school, lunchtime, or afterschool writing program. You may also set up writing clubs in your home, church, or community center. Check with your community education program for sources and resources. Some clubs, with members of various ages of students, meet together to share their writing and to produce magazines, books, or newspapers. Other clubs imitate adult writing groups by encouraging members to submit their writing for publication by outside sources. Check a current copy of the *Children's Writer's and Illustrator's Market,* as well as other resources described in Chapter 5. The main requirement for a student writing club is an interest in student writing and the ability to help students of different age levels interact productively in an enjoyable atmosphere.

If you are involved in a middle school or junior high parent-teacher organization or school advisory council, you may be in a position to recommend or help with the creation of a new class in the curriculum geared toward newspapers, creative writing, or researching for nonfiction articles. School officials may be willing to create a legitimate course when significant interest becomes apparent.

Working With Reluctant Teachers

If you are a parent who understands the importance of empowering approaches to writing instruction, and your child's teacher does not, your potential problem changes. If the teacher is heavily entrenched in traditional, rigid, and controlling approaches (such as an overemphasis on handwriting drills or insistence on teacher-assigned topics), and you wish to discuss this philosophy and your child's best welfare as a writer, the danger now becomes the teacher perceiving that you know more or think you know more than he or she does. If the sense of this threatens them, teachers likely will have reservations about inviting you into the classroom, or even into a discussion about what your child needs and deserves as a writer. Understandably, many teachers feel vulnerable and hesitant to expose themselves to the scrutiny of adults who they fear might criticize their methods and beliefs. Some teachers—most, in fact—worry that you might attempt to impose your ideas and tell them how to do their jobs. These problems can be solved and in many situations, prevented, if you can picture yourself validating the teacher for his or her attempts on behalf of your child, and then actually coaching the teacher to be who your gifted writer needs.

Coaching can be a form of cosupporting your child by providing resources, ideas, and support. Coaching allows you to take care of some classroom chores that require time and energy the teacher could otherwise spend in mentoring the writing process. Because coaching is traditionally considered to be a teaching or supervisory role, you will not likely be able to assume the role without having developed a reciprocally trusting relationship of respect and recognition of roles and responsibilities with the teacher. The relationship is the key, because coaching occurs only when you and the teacher put forth your best interpersonal selves. Hopefully, your attempts to support the teacher as a partner, or by functioning as an assistant coach, will not be the first exposure the teacher has had to this kind of experience with parental support. If the teacher has had little experience with parents who desire this level of involvement, you will need to work in a conditioning manner—patiently and gradually earning the teacher's trust.

From the parental side of this issue, it doesn't seem fair that we should have to teach the teachers how to work with us. The sad fact is, parent-teacher relationships are not addressed in most teacher education programs. This is an unfortunate paradox, because the most prevalent complaint of first-year and early-career teachers is that they do not know how to work with parents. Clashes between interpersonal styles, habits, and situations typically develop into situations ranging from no communication with home, to teachers preferring to work without parental input for classroom education, opting for simply giving parent-teacher conference reports, all the way to asking for home-based support for what goes on in the classroom. The influencing variables are personality styles and attitudes or a history of positive experiences with helpful parents.

Prickly Questions and Thorny Issues

What can we do about teachers who impose strict guidelines and rigid structures on children's writing instruction and assignments? What about teachers who cannot refrain from marking any misspelling or punctuation problems? What about teachers who insist that children write only to the prompts given to them, and refuse to allow children to write on their own topics and ideas? What do we do about a teacher who won't budge from her methods, even after we've coached her to the best of our abilities? If you believe, as I do, that the way writing is addressed in the classroom is as critical as any other element of your child's education, then the first reaction is pull your child from that classroom or school, and find an alternative situation. However, there is a lot at stake when we try this solution, and we cannot always choose both ends of the stick. In other words, consider your options thoroughly and wisely before you make a decision.

Getting Down to Brass Tacks

Today's educational climate is one of skepticism and self-doubt, causing us to only be able to hear faint echoes of strong and fearless voices advocating for the empowering teaching of writing and communication. In some ways, many teachers have been disempowered, and we can, perhaps, understand their reluctance to listen to every source that demands attention to another detail for which they thought they had ownership. Their fear of losing more ground may make them fearful or impatient. What if teaching writing the way we are expecting or requesting takes too long? A high stakes test or mandated proof of something measurable is always around the corner or lurking over their shoulders. As an involved parent, your have at least three options, any one of which could widen the gap between you and your child's teacher, or provide the encouragement and reinforcement that the teacher has longed for, and to which he will be receptive and grateful.

Opening Doors

Behind Door No. 1 is the attempt to arouse in the teacher his or her original beliefs in empowering possibilities for students. You may be the force who can reignite the spark for excellent teaching that was once there, to reintroduce the teacher to that small, quiet place within her where she can escape the nagging feelings of doubt that have undermined her effectiveness for some time. This situation is only possible when you can start from a foundation of time, patience, and security.

Your foundation will be comprised of your knowledge that you are meeting your child's needs, for the time being, by what you have provided at home or outside resources you have tapped. This will allow you to see the class writing time as, at worst, a waste of time, but at best, *some* exposure to *some* part of your child's literacy awareness. Through your conversations, both scheduled and

> The teacher needs to see clearly that your motives are to appreciatively and knowledgeably stand behind and support him, not tear him down or assert control over his responsibilities.

unplanned opportunities, or in sincere, well-reasoned, affirming correspondence, you can appeal to the teacher's sense of dignity for self and for the students. The teacher needs to see clearly that your motives are to appreciatively and knowledgeably stand behind and support him, not tear him down or assert control over his responsibilities. As the teacher comes to trust you and senses that your esteem for him is growing, this can be reciprocated, and changes in his delivery and expectations in the classroom can effectively occur. However, this kind of win-win circumstance is a case-by-case phenomenon and there are no guarantees that it will be achieved. It is certain that if this kind of trusting climate cannot be realized, this option is not likely to be effective for you or your child.

Door No. 2 contains the option to chalk up this school year to the misfortunate luck of the draw, and simply focus all of your efforts on how to meet your child's needs at home and through available outside resources. While it may appear that this option is a resignation to an unalterable and dysfunctional system, it can be the most peaceful route, and can raise powerful questions to school board and other governing bodies who will, in the future, require the desired changes to occur. Documenting all of your efforts to provide for your child's writing needs, as well as indications of your child's progress and accomplishment, may prove useful for your future efforts, or those of others who choose Door No. 1.

Door No. 3 is opened by degrees. Opening it just a crack would include your attempts to make your child's teacher aware of the negative effects of some of the individual parts of the teacher's instruction, assignments, and assessments. Your entrance through this door will include your active response to your child's discouragement over returned papers covered with red pen, her inability to produce original writing, or her complete distaste for writing, associated with a didactic or overcontrolled time of the school day. If your child is too young to approach the teacher herself, or lacks the knowledge of how things should be, your choice may be to make the teacher aware of how your child has been negatively affected by the teacher's methods. You can approach the teacher, initially, with offers to have professional writers that you know serve as guest speakers in the classroom. A very well-delivered and compelling case for the types of writing support that have worked for a professional writer may inspire the willingness of a teacher to investigate ways to change what he or she has been doing.

Real change is very difficult. The teacher's response may not be what you would desire (although you may have the fortune of working with a willing and obliging teacher). The situation in the classroom may improve. It may stay the same or it may deteriorate. Your ultimate choice may be to determine if one of the other teachers of that course or grade level could provide improved writing instruction. If that is an option that you can make happen with positive outcomes, you will know that you have entered the right door for you and your child. You would not be the first parent who removed your child from a classroom or school because teachers were unable to provide the proper experiences and environment needed. Changing your child's classroom placement is extremely complicated, and if you determine this to be your best option, you will want to make sure that the ultimate results are truly in the best interest of your child.

In the best of all worlds, you won't have to choose any of these doors. The optimal situation is one where your child's teachers have been open to changes in teaching methods, have come to understand that the human spirit of creativity is alive in some way in every child, and have been able to retain their belief in the voices that led them to their calling to be teachers in the first place.

The Writing Workshop in the Classroom

A writing workshop provides an environment where the child can acquire and grow in his or her skills of writing, along with developing the fluency, confidence, ability to make and record observations, and the desire to see him- or herself as a writer. Writing workshops are also optimal frameworks for motivating students to meaningfully learn and practice the writing conventions we want them to know.

Maine teacher Nancie Atwell coined the term *writers' workshop* in 1987 to reflect the busy and engaging nature of a comprehensive writing curriculum. A writers' workshop has several components: self-selected writing, minilessons, conferences, revision decisions, group sharing, and editing conferences, both with peers and with the teacher or "editor in chief." In the classroom, a writing workshop creates an environment where students can acquire all of the subskills that make up the phenomenon of writing. Children are taught some specific but interchangeable stages of the writing process, which they can then track and plan. Typical stages are listed below, but they vary according to teachers' preferences and philosophy or training.

Typical Stages in a Writing Workshop

The following are the typical stages in a writers' workshop; however, they do not necessarily have to be completed in the order listed below.

- *Prewriting,* or thinking about how to tell a story or capture an idea;
- *Drafting,* or writing the idea down for the first time, focusing on the story or content;
- *Minilessons,* or instruction in a small or large group setting that is responsive to the immediate or present questions and/ or needs of the current writing projects;
- *Conferences,* or meetings between one student and a teacher, or one student and a peer, or a very small group of peers, to discuss the progress of a piece of writing, or new ideas for the direction of the writing;
- *Revising,* or making changes through adding and cutting details or clarifying ideas through changing words, whole paragraphs, or even the order in which ideas occur in the story, poem, or article;
- *Sharing,* or presenting the writing to a group or whole class of peers, and usually receiving feedback and suggestions;

- *Editing,* or attending to writing conventions, such as spelling or grammatical errors, punctuation, or formatting issues; and
- *Publishing,* or putting some type of closure on the story, poem, article, or book. It may be a decision to place the piece of writing in its unfinished form into a folder to keep and later prioritize. Publishing may, however, be some form of public display as a way to share the writing with the intended audience.

The order of the stages in a writing workshop can be switched around, or some can be skipped for some projects and expanded for others. In some classrooms, the teacher attempts to assign work to the entire class so that all students are working on the same stages at one time. However, this is not optimal workshop practice. It is more advisable to guide the students to move freely and independently, but responsibly, from stage to stage, making decisions about their writing along the way.

The writing workshop allows each child to acquire and develop writing skills and knowledge on his or her individual timeline. This is an important factor in the education of the child who emerges as a particularly gifted writer, usually chronologically or skillfully ahead of his same-age peers.

The term *workshop* may conjure up memories of a laid-back feeling of permissiveness, reminiscent of the 1970s. Some teachers fear the idea and the term, which may suggest to them chaos and noise, with students wandering around without purpose. Actually, a writing workshop is a purposeful learning environment with a validating guidance system that produces a student-centered, productive, and positive place to learn.

Observing an appropriate writing workshop in action reveals a roomful of young writers engaged in the act of composing, revising, publishing, and sharing—all on topics that have become important and meaningful to them. You will find teachers beginning or ending the workshop periods by gathering all or small groups of the students together for short lessons, or for some kind of sharing time. But, at the core of an appropriate workshop, students are making decisions about their thoughts and ideas, and then putting their words on paper.

An excellent source for creating the optimal writing workshop in a classroom is Ralph Fletcher's and JoAnn Portalupi's *Writing Workshop: The Essential Guide* (2001). Their analogy illuminates a conceivable portrait of how this looks, sounds, and feels in a classroom:

> We might clarify our thinking about the writing workshop by considering the conditions present when kids learn other tasks. Take skiing, for instance. Our kids had never skied before. We drove them to the mountain, bought lift tickets, rented equipment, and paid for them to have a lesson. (Ouch!) I can still see our boys standing there, cold and forlorn, waiting for the ski lesson to begin. From their body language it was painfully apparent how uncomfortable and awkward they felt. The lesson began. By midmorning they had mastered snowplowing, and by lunch they had each gone down one of the intermediate trails. We were amazed at how quickly they transformed themselves into skiers. How did it happen? When we looked closer, and reflected on the instructors who worked with our kids, several things stood out:
>
> 1. They were all skiers themselves. They wore that ultra-cool skiing apparel, talked the talk, and radiated contagious enthusiasm for the sport.

2. They believed in doing as opposed to talking. They didn't begin their lessons with a lecture, ski video, or ski simulator. They helped our kids step into their bindings and immediately got them skiing.

3. They expected plenty of failure. "You're all going to fall a lot today," one of the instructors said with a rueful smile. "Everybody does. You'll probably be pretty sore tonight. But I guarantee you this: by the end of today you'll be skiing."

4. They built on strengths: "You're doing it! You're telling me this is your first time? I can't believe that! You're skiing like a pro!"

The writing workshop strives to create hothouse conditions where our students can thrive as writers. (Fletcher & Portalupi, 2001, pp. 4–5. Reprinted with permission.)

A well-done writing workshop requires a significant shift in the philosophy of classroom organization, and can be a significant aid in the discovery and development of exceptional writers. The writing workshop does not place the teacher at center stage. Rather, he or she sets up the structure, allows students plenty of choice, and offers students an abundance of support, guidance, resources, and mentorship. Once the structures and supports are understood, students are given the freedom to work at their own pace (as long as they *are working*), and to write about whatever they want. Students are supported in their choices of writing topics by minilessons where brainstorming and the conceptualization of writing projects occur. The focus is on student-led and student-centered writing success.

Students in one classroom may be working at any given stage of the process, but they are all working at writing. Some stages of the writing process are skipped by some students at some times, depending on the topic and the students' chosen audiences or purposes. For instance, one student or a group of students working on a special book to be presented and read to a classroom of younger students will want to carefully select their topic, receive minilessons from the teacher that are specific to the type of book or story they are creating, revise after receiving feedback from other groups of their peers, and publish in a permanent method that takes several hours over several days. At the same time, individual students may be experimenting with a particular writing style and choose not to publish this attempt. The progression is flexible, individual, and accommodating to a positive classroom climate for a great diversity of learning styles, cultural preferences, and writing abilities.

National Support for Teaching Writing Authentically

As a promoter of a nationwide initiative to improve the teaching of writing in schools, the National Writing Project (NWP) sponsors educational research and fosters leadership and programs that will help students become successful writers and learners. The basic premise of the NWP is that every student deserves a highly skilled teacher of writing, and improves the reality of that through its programs. NWP sites are located on university campuses and serve more than 100,000 teachers annually, with the goal of placing the writing project within reach of every teacher in America. The NWP Web site (http://www.writing project.org/) includes a version of Table 6, which describes the differences between a traditional, assignment-based classroom

Table 6 **Characteristics of Classrooms When Writing Is** **Assigned and When Writing Is Taught**	
When Writing Is Assigned	**When Writing Is Taught**
Students are asked to write only on the topics teachers give them.	Students have opportunities to create and choose topics that matter to them.
The teacher selects writing topics without consideration of the potential audience and purpose.	The paper's audience and purpose are specifically identified in assignments.
The teacher spends most of her time correcting papers.	The teacher spends most of her time teaching writing skills and strategies.
Students are asked to analyze, compare, describe, narrate, review, and summarize, without knowing or learning the strategies to successfully complete these tasks.	Students are given and taught to use writing models, assignments, and strategies to guide each writing task.
Students are not aware of significant improvement in their writing.	Students reflect on significant growth—or lack of it—in their specific writing skills.
Students are required to rewrite—in some cases. But, such rewriting usually is limited to correcting grammar, usage, and other writing conventions.	Students are encouraged to revise, edit, and improve their work—and to correct drafts and then resubmit the work.
Students are required to write without much forethought.	Students think about what they write through brainstorming, freewriting, role-playing, discussion, or other prewriting activities.
Students and teachers are bored by what students write.	Students and teachers are excited about what students write and make efforts to display and publish it.

Note. Adapted from National Writing Project, 2005.

and a classroom where writing is authentically taught, such as writing workshop classrooms.

The National Council of Teachers of English (NCTE), in conjunction with two other accrediting and literacy-based organizations has published standards concerning the instruction of literacy. Those specifically addressing writing are concerned with students adjusting their use of language for effective communication with a variety of audiences for a variety of purposes. They emphasize the employment of a wide range of strategies and the use of different and appropriate writing process elements, participating as knowledgeable, reflective, creative, and critical members of a variety of literacy communities. And, finally, NCTE standards suggest students learn to communicate effectively for their own purposes, including learning, enjoyment, and persuasion.

There is a good chance that your child's teacher knows about or has heard of the National Writing Project, and would respond positively to a conversation about its goals. A copy of the NCTE standards are likely within reach of every teacher, even if some are not aware of them. In fact, the basal and commercial text programs from which many teachers draw their material have been written in accordance with national standards and widely accepted best practices as a focus. Unfortunately, it seems that our children are often at the mercy of the luck of the draw in each grade level and school when it comes to learning from a teacher who thoughtfully plans instruction and believes in empowering students. Even within the same school, and in some cases, the same grade level, some teachers are either unable to function in the choice, support, and accountability necessary in writing workshops or simply choose to control writing processes in the more traditional, didactic sense. Chapter 4 addresses how parents and other out-of-school support persons can approximate the processes and benefits of a writing workshop. If your child's

teacher is not knowledgeable about writing workshop philosophy, or unwilling to facilitate writing workshop in the classroom,
you may choose to seek an alternative that allows you to provide
the appropriate environment and motivation.

Alternative Schooling Choices

There are alternatives for public schooling that address the
needs of gifted writers. The growing number of charter schools
in the country reflects a need for addressing a variety of academic
needs in alternative ways. Magnet schools appeal to parents who
wish their children's education to be focused on specific areas of
the curricula, and some great writing programs can be found in
some magnet schools. Again, private schools are a possibility,
but the writing instruction is not any more consistent among
and between these alternative forms of education than in public
schools. In fact, many schools and programs in private, charter, or
magnet schools are instigated because of a local or regional trend
to have teachers go back to the basics. Be sure to understand what
that phrase suggests about literacy instruction, because it may
mean going back all the way to rigid, controlling, and overstruc-
tured writing.

Another positive option may be the opportunity to supple-
ment your child's public school learning with distance education,
advanced college writing programs, or college and high school
concurrent enrollment courses. Secondary level Advanced
Placement (AP) courses and honors classes may be positive
options for your child, but again, you will want to investigate the
specific philosophical foundation of the curriculum or the back-
ground of the teacher assigned to those programs. At any school
level, acceleration may be possible, allowing your child to attend

a writing class that is advanced beyond the grade level where your child is working. Because parents' requests for advancement are often met by school officials with hesitancy (some teachers are not fond of parents suggesting that they are unable to meet their children's needs, and may take a defensive stance), you may be met with a requirement that outlines a difficult process of proving your child's ability and academic need. This option will be much easier if you can work with a gifted education specialist to navigate the process of setting it in place for your child. A call to the school district to request the name of its coordinator for gifted education should yield an advocate for you and your child.

Chapter 4

What You Can Do at Home for Your Gifted Writer

I won't go so far as to say that families who ignore or devalue the uses and worth of writing in the home constitute cases of flawed kinship. But I will argue that writing should lie at the heart of any family . . .
—Peter Stillman, 1989

L et's say you have decided that arriving at a consensus with the school or your child's teacher about what your child needs as a writer is an insurmountable task. Perhaps you have recognized that the school requirements or teacher's methods will not appropriately enhance your child's needs for finding, developing, and expressing his or her sense of self, relationships, and the world. Perhaps you simply desire to take a very active support role at home to enrich your child's writing development and achievement.

One young writer knows firsthand the benefit of having support for his writing at home. Christopher Paolini was 15 when he began his novel, *Eragon*. It was published when he was 18, and instantly became a *New York Times* bestseller. By the time Paolini was 20 (in February of 2004), it had been on the best-selling list for 26 weeks, and was the No. 1 best-selling children's chapter book at the time. On his Web site (http://www.alagaesia.com), Paolini attributes his success to his mother, a former Montessori teacher and children's book author, who homeschooled Christopher and his sister. Christopher (2005) explains,

> Aside from textbook lessons, she had us perform many exercises designed to stimulate our creativity. Even at a young age I enjoyed writing short stories and poems. . . . All I really wanted to do was share the epics floating around in my head with other people—writing was just something I had to master in order to make those sagas reality. (¶ 7, 8)

Whether you have opted for homeschooling, home reinforcement, or home enrichment, there are many resources available to you. You may find that these options not only provide the support your child needs as a writer, but they may also deepen and strengthen your relationship with your child.

Gifted Basics: What Your Gifted Writer Needs

In Chapter 5, you will be introduced to some programs and specific curricula that may work well for you. But, first, it is important that you see the development of your child's writing not so much as a curriculum or program, but rather, as a *vision*—a way of looking at his or her writing that takes both of you right inside the process itself. Your child may already feel this way about writing, and may talk about himself as a writer, or about wanting to be an author. For some children, writing becomes the heart and soul of their being. They have tasted the thrill of putting their words on a page and they have noticed how their words evoke certain emotions and reactions from their readers.

If you have seen this kind of passion in your child, then you must ask yourself: *What makes writing work for my child?* Answering this question will likely lead you to ask your child how he or she feels about his or her writing *process*. Really listening to your child's answers and combining it with your own observations will lead you to know how to be your child's best mentor, and how to do it with all your heart. That kind of mentoring is simple when you narrow down the components of what gifted writers do, what they need, and what they deserve. In this chapter, I will outline the kinds of behaviors and attitudes that you will want to engender and support, some general "how to" instructions for creating a home-based writing workshop, and some ideas for inspiring the desire to write. Be careful, though! You and the rest of your family may become dedicated, passionate authors, as well.

> For some children, writing becomes the heart and soul of their being. They have tasted the thrill of putting their words on a page and they have noticed how their words evoke certain emotions and reactions from their readers.

Here are some behaviors and attitudes you will want to engender and support:

- Your child taking charge of his own writing process.
- Your child understanding the differences between strong and weak writing, and using that knowledge to write stronger drafts.
- Your child revising and editing his own writing because he *wants* to make it better, and knows what to do about it.

This should not sound like magic. It should make complete sense, based on what you have already noticed about your child's abilities, desires, and behaviors. These are the keys to unlocking the door to your writer. When your child is empowered to see himself as a writer, he becomes an assessor of his own work. He will become much less dependent on you to give him a specific assignment. Writing is mostly creative problem solving, after all. He cannot get better at it if someone else is always solving the problems for him. In *Creating Writers Through 6-Trait Writing Assessment and Instruction,* Vicki Spandel (2005b) quotes a young student writer: "I write because I like hearing the river of words flow like the ocean, so smooth and graceful. I like to read it over and over until the words ask me to stop" (p. 63).

Your goal in mentoring and supporting your gifted writer will be to help him assess his own and others' writing, talk about his own and other's writing, focus on his own strengths and problems, and use literature and discussion as models of what to do or not do. You must empower him to take charge of his own writing process and learn to be an independent problem solver.

Paulette Wasserstein (1995), found that 11- to 13-year-olds learned best when they were challenged, actively engaged, and asked to be self-reflective. Self-reflection is best developed when the child's opinion is validated with discussion that communicates to her your interest and respect more than your knowledge about what is right or desirable. If your child can engage in reflective processes with another child or two, the social aspects of this process will be even greater. It removes you from the constant role of literary critic and allows you to be a true mentor. If you are the only one who reads your child's work and comments on it, your relationship, as well as her motivation to write, may suffer. The emerging or developing desire to write may suffer from too much criticism from you, even if that criticism is given only for the writing. Parent-child relationships are notorious for provoking misperceptions about unconditional acceptance and love. Even if your child seeks your judgment of her writing, she will always want the security of your love and acceptance first and foremost. It takes a high level of emotional maturity for your daughter to perceive that your criticism is of her work, not her true self. It is often difficult to develop the ability to differentiate between one's writing and one's self as a person.

Damage to parent-child relationships can also develop from insincere or nonspecific praise for writing. Praise can become tiresome and can remove the innate rewards your child might attain from her writing process. Being on the receiving end of all praise, especially unspecific praise ("I like it! That is so interesting!"), is emotionally draining and disempowering. By contrast, it feels good to your child to know that you value her opinions or her questions about her own writing. When she sees that it is more important to you to hear what *she* thinks or questions about her writing than for you to give your opinion or teach her from your store of knowledge, she develops the ability to think independently, to become literate about standards of good writing, and to feel that her opinions have purpose. Mem Fox (1993), the prolific children's author and teacher, wrote,

> Many of my teacher education students, after twelve years at school, come to me helpless and fearful as writers, detesting it in the main, believing that they can't write because they have nothing to say because they haven't cared about saying anything because it hasn't mattered, because there's been no real investment for so long." (p. 21)

Your mentoring will also become invaluable to your child if you engage in some of the writing yourself, and demonstrate that there are worthy purposes in the act of writing. My biggest complaint about classroom writing is that so much of the process revolves around busywork, or unauthentic writing. If you seek to simply recreate what happens in a classroom, you run the danger of engendering in your child feelings of stress and boredom rather than compelling excitement and self-fulfillment. Wasserstein (1995) found what we have all suspected, that "hard work does not turn students away, but busywork destroys them" (p. 43). You will find a variety of ideas to use yourself, with your child, or with your whole family in the last section of this chapter. In order for these ideas to be inspiring experiences rather than busywork, it will be important for you and your child to select ideas that will feel authentic to his or her tastes and interests. You may want to consider your own home version of a writing workshop, because it validates your child's interest, and sets up a system that will allow you both to feel like much can be accomplished. Writing should not feel like dreaded homework, but rather, it should seem like official and important business that is also enjoyable. A writing workshop can enhance your parent-child relationship, and that is, perhaps, the best result of both of your efforts.

> If you seek to simply recreate what happens in a classroom, you run the danger of engendering in your child feelings of stress and boredom rather than compelling excitement and self-fulfillment.

A Writing Workshop in the Home

Take a Lesson From Good Writing Workshops

A writing workshop in a classroom strives to create conditions where students can thrive as writers, at their own pace, mingled with appropriate challenges and prompts from their mentors. You can provide optimal writing workshop conditions for your writer at home by allowing plenty of choice and inspiration, and by offering an abundance of resources, support, discussion, guidance, and mentorship. One reason that the writing workshop is such a natural fit in the home is that it creates a sense of responsibility and provides your child with opportunities to interact with you and the rest of the family for ideas and feedback. For some parents, the most difficult part of teaching writing is getting used to releasing a large amount of control in order to gently guide your child toward independence. Isn't that one of the greatest challenges of parenthood anyway? The journey to becoming an independent writer can be very pleasant and compelling, as you and your child will build your relationship with each other through writing experiences. By the end of the journey, you will find that somewhere along the way, there was an invisible, but reciprocal, transfer of inspiration, desire, passion, and intellectual self-confidence.

Some changes to your routine or your beliefs about homework that are required in order to provide a true writing workshop at home may not be easy at first. They will require you to find new ways to organize the time you and your child have together. Also, the act of gathering and organizing materials that will entice your child to write can be time-consuming and constantly expanding. You may even find that you and your child will benefit from subtle or major changes that affect the inspirational and creative atmosphere in your home. The fact that you are reading this book suggests that your desires for your child and the atmosphere in your home are already ripe for a true writing workshop.

Ultimately, you will find it worth your time and effort, because homework time or daily reading sessions will be transformed into time that both you and your child look forward to as he becomes passionate about writing.

Workshop is a word that suggests a setting in which artists or craftsmen are involved in a variety of hands-on, creative activities. The workshop leader does very little up-front lecturing. Think of writing time as a workshop where your child, like an artist, crafts his individual works over time. A workshop is also interactive, because receiving feedback gives the writer the impetus to keep going out of a desire to write and to improve his craft.

Some much needed workshop components include:

- *Organization and accessibility of writing materials.* You need to keep a wide choice of writing tools and a variety of different sizes and colors of paper, lined and unlined, within free and easy reach of the child. Publishing materials are an important part of this collection, so you might include scissors, tape, a stapler, a hole-punch, yarn or ribbon, peel-off letters, and cardboard and cardstock for making book covers.
- *Writing resources.* Keep a dictionary and a thesaurus and other word collections or grammar and usage handbooks, according to appropriate ability levels, placed where your child can access them easily when he wants information. You may also want to have on hand a collection of picture books whose design or text have inspired your child, short story anthologies for learning about writers' techniques, and non-fiction books and materials that serve as sources and models for information on topics of interest. Your child may also enjoy file folders or paper trays for keeping ongoing projects in sight or for filing them away.
- *A place to write.* This can be as simple or as complex as you and your child wish it to be. It may start with a simple desk or place at a table already in your home, and then evolve into an elaborate office that inspires your child—an area that the two of you have planned and discussed as your child spends more and more time as a writer. Be sure to have this writing place

reflect the style and personality of your child. Include easy access to writing materials and tools (paper, writing utensils, filing boxes, or drawers) and a comfortable chair. With your child, choose artwork or posters that inspire him. If he is already wired to computer work, include easy access to a computer, printer, and even a scanner. Of course, computer equipment is not necessary, and really only advisable if you already know that your child is motivated by it and possesses some aptitude with it.

* *Rituals and routines.* These should be very different in your home than they would be in a classroom. Much of what is done in classrooms occurs because of classroom and behavior management issues, or because of a teacher's or students' noise intolerance. This reveals the assigned nature of writing in many classrooms, and a regression to reliance on traditional methods of rigidly assessed writing, rather than the choice and responsibility of true workshops. You may find that your child responds to simple routines that he or she enjoys on a regular basis, such as dad reading the child's newest story every Sunday evening, or the child sharpening and replacing pencils and pens every Monday morning. Your child may even initiate some kind of checklist for herself, enjoying a sense of achievement for checking off items as she accomplishes them. Having a specific plan for how the workshop time will be spent is a personal decision that will be unique according to your child's personality and preferences. You will find many ideas in the list of resources below.

Choices for writing experiences and topics can, of course, come from you and your child brainstorming lists of issues that are important to the two of you and goals you both set for his or her future. Is she interested in history and politics, or science and the future of genetics? Is he fascinated by the arts, or by the lives of athletes? Any area of interest and wonder can provide a wealth of subject areas and topics to inspire, motivate, and engage the young writer. Resources are right beneath your fingertips on the Internet, in your local library, and even in your home library. Technology has made library resources readily available to even the most remote locations in the United States and Canada. Your support, guidance, and mentorship are discussed below, but in addition to what you can provide as a loving and caring parent, consider finding an outside mentor for your child, and if possible, a small, peer-based writing group.

Resources for Developing a Writing Workshop at Home

The way you actually set up your writing workshop should feel completely comfortable to you and your child. You certainly don't want to escape from a rigid structure in a classroom, only to defeat your goals by initiating inappropriate structures at home. There is really no right way to do this, but reading about what some teachers have done in classrooms with children who are the same age as your child can give you ideas for how to approach specific tasks and what to try first. The following resources can help you as you formulate your own ideas for setting up a writing workshop in your home that is just right for you and your child.

- *Writing Workshop: The Essential Guide* by Ralph Fletcher and JoAnn Portalupi, published in 2001. Fletcher and Portalupi are husband-and-wife writers who are both passionate about what young writers need. Their suggestions are easy to picture for yourself, and practical enough to adapt to your home use. As you read this book you will find that it validates your desire to provide this environment for your child.

- *About the Authors: Writing Workshop With Our Youngest Writers* by Katie Wood Ray with Lisa B. Cleaveland, published in 2004. Ray beautifully describes young children in the act of learning, and demonstrates how to nourish writing right from the start. She gives step-by-step explanations on how to set up and maintain a writing workshop, and details 11 units of study. This book also includes many examples of short books by young children. While the book targets classrooms for young children, the underlying principles and main points are absolutely applicable to a parent seeking to nurture his or her child's writing life.
- *Scaffolding Young Writers: A Writers' Workshop Approach* by Linda J. Dorn and Carla Soffos, published in 2001. Dorn and Soffos have produced a clear roadmap for organizing a workshop approach to writing with young children that includes an overview of how children become writers, analyses of students' writing samples, checklists and benchmark behaviors, and completion checklists. One feature is a detailed chapter on organizing writing workshops, with information on materials, routines, and procedures.
- *What You Know by Heart: How to Develop Curriculum for Your Writing Workshop* by Katie Wood Ray, published in 2002. While this book is addressed to teachers, the diligent and sincere parent or mentor will find it invaluable in knowing how to empower and inspire the gifted writer, while the child learns and grows in her development as a writer.
- Scholastic's Web site, *Writing Workshop: Oral History* (http://teacher.scholastic.com/activities/writing). This Web site provides a very specific outline of a writing workshop project. The outline can be used generically as a guideline for developing the components of a home writing workshop, with suggestions about sequencing daily activities.

Finding a Mentor for Your Child

Ideas for possible mentors are limitless. Two major characteristics to be concerned about in finding an outside mentor for your child are that he is willing to become involved in your child's writing development, and that he possesses some kind of credible writing experience that can be respected and admired by your child. The first requirement, willingness, can only be ascertained by your approaching and discussing the request with possible candidates. Second, credible writers can come from numerous sources, such as college professors, newspaper reporters or editors, high school writing teachers, college students enrolled in writing classes, published authors who live in your local area (librarians are usually familiar with the local authors), and neighbors who do a little writing and a lot of reading. Consider getting well-acquainted with local librarians. They are usually the best-read members of your community, and have developed a keen sense of quality. They can help provide many examples of great writing, keep you and your child aware of events that occur for the interest of writers and authors, and open up a whole world of support and resources to you both. With or without a separate mentor (besides yourself), the following ideas can facilitate you in providing the nurturing environment your young writer needs.

Working With a Mentor

If the idea of having an outside mentor for your child appeals to you, you probably already have some ideas for whom you would like to approach. Because acceptance of your request will require the mentor to give you and your child some of his spare time, you will want to present your request in an unassuming way. Let the mentor know early in the conversation what types of reasonable compensation you are willing to provide. This can include, but is not restricted to, a monetary fee. It may be that you could provide childcare, or some other service such as sewing, word processing, painting, or cooking. Be creative, and be open to some creative or unique ideas from the mentor.

At first, ask for a minimal amount of the mentor's time. Your child probably doesn't have a track record where writing is concerned, so one short session every month is a logical place to start. If the relationship is productive and mutually satisfying, the mentor will probably suggest a new schedule. Whether the mentor is a longtime friend, close acquaintance, or someone referred to you by another source, you should be present during the initial sessions. If you determine together that your child might respond better to the mentor with you not in the same room, you can eventually set up a public location (e.g., the school or public library, community center, church fellowship hall), or a place where you or other family members are close at hand.

If you find someone willing to mentor your child, but she is uncertain as to what she should do during the mentoring session, suggest that she have your child read her writing aloud and then give the child feedback, and have the mentor share with the child some aspect of her writing craft. Consider discussing the possibility of the mentor "thinking aloud" with your child. This would include the mentor reading aloud some of her writing, verbally asking the questions she would normally ask herself, and talking aloud about her possible solutions and decisions. Ultimately, the mentoring relationship is one of reciprocal sharing and feedback.

Some Web sites listed in Chapter 5 include online mentoring services for a fee. You may also set up your own e-mail mentoring process between your child and the mentor, which could be safely read and facilitated by you. This type of situation appeals to many authors because they can fit it into their personal schedules. Writing tutors can be contracted in similar circumstances, but the purpose and focus of a tutor would be different than that of a mentor. A mentor's goals will develop gradually over time based on what skills she sees, and what she senses about the next step she wants the writer to try, whereas a tutor's goals are straightforward from the beginning—to improve general knowledge, skills, and understanding of a topic.

Being Your Child's Mentor

My attempts to mentor my oldest daughter when she was a 6-year-old always ended in tears for both of us. Somehow, we always ended our sessions with unrealized expectations and feelings of disappointment. As much as I knew about this little beginning writer, and as much as I desired to be a validating, emotional support to her, we never got to a true reciprocal place. I suppose we were both entrenched in other roles with each other. You may find your situation similar to ours. On the other

> Your role [as a mentor] should be shaped by an attitude and philosophy, as well as a concern for helping your child grow as a writer.

hand, you may be the very best person to mentor your child. My son and I easily fell into a mentoring relationship that we were able to turn on when we wanted to work on it, and turn off when we went back to functioning as mother and son. Ask your child for suggestions about who he would like to have as his mentor. If you are the answer, be willing to learn a new way of relating to him during your mentoring sessions. Your role should be shaped by an attitude and philosophy, as well as a concern for helping your child grow as a writer. The following resources can help you form a mentoring attitude and philosophy.

- *Creative Power: The Nature and Nurture of Children's Writing* by Ronald Cramer, published in 2001. In very inspirational ways, Cramer explores strategies and practices for understanding young writers and writing, with strong emphasis on the creative capabilities of children. This book is addressed to teachers in classrooms, but Cramer's ideas and beliefs about children's writing will inspire true mentorship for involved parents.
- *What a Writer Needs* by Ralph Fletcher, published in 1993. This one is for you, the mentor, rather than the writer. It's packed with inspiring advice that is wise, practical, and memorable. You *can* be the mentor your child needs.
- *Wondrous Words: Writers and Writing in the Elementary Classroom* by Katie Wood Ray, published in 1999. Ray inspires all who would mentor children with her gentle approach of sharing the best in children's literature with children, and then helping them determine what makes that literature wondrous. She describes how to inspire children to seek that kind of wonderment in their own writing.
- *Writing Toward Home: Tales and Lessons to Find Your Way* by Georgia Heard, published in 1995. This book probably comes the closest to a session-by-session sequence for mentoring discussions and activities. By reminding you that the true source of writing is your creative self, this book will help you find your writing voice, and help your child find his or hers. Most of all, this book will make you want to write.

Help Your Child Take Charge of His Own Writing Process

In Chapter 3, the idea of a student writing club was introduced as a potential noon hour or afterschool activity. A children's writing club is certainly something that you and your child may be interested in initiating at home, separate from school activities. Check with your local library to see if any children's writing clubs already exist in your community, and how to become a participant. If none exists, your local library may be willing to support you and your child in its initiation in a variety of ways, such as providing a meeting place, advertising as part of the library community outreach methods, and pointing out the published resources and local author workshops available to you through the library.

Together, read any of the resource publications annotated at the end of this chapter, as well as those in Chapter 5. A specific recommendation is to read together one of Ralph Fletcher's brief and inexpensive paperbacks, *A Writer's Notebook: Unlocking the Writer Within* (1996), *Live Writing: Breathing Life Into Your Words* (1999), or *How Writer's Work: Finding a Process That Works For You* (2000). Shop together for a writer's notebook, and get one for both of you. Have your child consider and tell you what kind of place or surroundings he or she would like to have to write in. Set up his or her personal writing space and encourage experimentation with a set time of day dedicated to writing. Find practical dictionaries and a thesaurus, as well as Web site resources for words and ideas. The following are some resources to help your child see him- or herself as a writer:

- *Live Writing: Breathing Life Into Your Words* by Ralph Fletcher, published in 1999. This small paperback is written to the child, and introduces the reader to writer's tools for making his words jump right off the page and into the heart of the reader.

- *How Writers Work: Finding a Process That Works for You* by Ralph Fletcher, published in 2000. Another small, inexpensive paperback, written to the child, this describes how writers work and how your child can make words do what he or she wants them to do.

- *Write Where You Are: How to Use Writing to Make Sense of Your Life: A Guide For Teens* by Caryn Mirriam-Goldberg, published in 1999. This creative writing guide also serves as self-help for teens, with writing exercises designed to get young people to know and like themselves while learning the craft of writing. Its conversational tone is inspiring for teens who are interested in writing and willing (or even reluctant) to give it a try.

Help Your Child Develop the Ability to Judge Strong and Weak Writing

To do this, you will want to know how to recognize it yourself—not just the mistakes, but the moments of wonder, detail, and magic. We must be able to communicate our ideas and listen to our children's ideas. Then, we must make our children partners, rather than recipients or victims, in assessing and responding to writing. We should seek their full participation and encourage them to set their own standards for their work. We should inspire them to learn how to think critically about writing. If you are constantly on the lookout for brilliant flashes of wonder (the golden lines or golden passages mentioned earlier in this book), you'll have fodder for many conversations with clear examples.

Keep your eyes open, as well, for books that may have been self-published (ask librarians or bookstore owners for titles and authors), or small newspapers and newsletters for examples of both good and bad writing. There are many examples out there of poor sentence structure, boring presentation of stories, or repetitive phrases and passages. In pointing out the weaknesses (or having your child discover them), refrain from belittling the writer or poking fun at the intellectual levels suggested by the writing.

A negative perception could be a red flag to a reluctant child that would prevent him from taking the risk to write his ideas and share them with you. Instead, ask questions and make comments that allow your child to suggest what the writer could have done instead, and what the outcome may have been.

Read Like a Writer

Constantly link reading and writing in both of your lives by reading like a writer, and encouraging your child to do the same. Writers read differently than people who don't write. We just do. The world is full of writing that makes us stop and take a second look. We read something and think, "Ooh . . . look at that. I need to show my son. That's really good writing." Because writing is something we do, we see possibilities for our own work every time we look closely at the work of other writers. Writers can't help but notice how things are written as they read because every encounter with a written text is an opportunity to learn our craft. Frankly, if you have recognized talent in your child's writing ability or even just his writing potential, and if you have purchased this book with the commitment to do something to help his writing processes, you may be a budding writer yourself. You certainly are a natural writing mentor. Finding snippets of good writing to share with your child will come naturally to you. And, when you happen upon some really good writing, you have to gather it for your child. Collect magazines, newspapers, memos, novels, billboard messages, e-mail messages, lyrics, letters, poems, and short stories. Every time you see writing, you are seeing something that will help you teach your child about good writing. Be constantly on the lookout for interesting ways to approach writing, such as sentence crafting, paragraph instruction, and techniques for making time move, getting a point across, or bringing characters to life. When you read, always be on the lookout for interesting things you might share with your child.

Discuss Different Models of Writing

In addition to gathering good pieces of writing, you should provide and consistently talk about models of good writing. Share with your child not only what your favorite texts are, but what you *think* and *feel* about them, as well. Let authors coteach with you. You can know these authors' work by heart, and you can return to them again and again to share with your child styles they may try in their writing. Have your child help you develop a list of things you both notice and talk about in the texts that you share. Create a list of "books we like, and why we like them." (You may be interested in starting a small collection of *bad* writing examples, as well. You can get some suggestions from children's librarians or children's literature textbooks. Unfortunately, it may not be difficult to develop at least a short list of didactic or condescending writing that has been published.) When reading together, play a game to find passages where the word choice is unique, or the voice of the author jumps right off the page. The best way to get started noticing good writing is to reread the texts you know and love, and then ask each other, "What is it that the writer is doing here?" Slow down your reading and think like a writer. Trust good authors to show you and your child how to write well.

Encourage Your Child to Write Like a Reader

When you read your child's writing, comment on the content first, always. Encourage him to listen to you read his writing, and to tell you how *he* likes the sound of his own writing. Respond to your child's writing clearly and simply by what you know about writing as a *reader* and a *writer*, not as a teacher or a critic. He will learn to write and rewrite with his ears and heart, which is the best you can hope to inspire in an avid writer. Casually challenge him or her to try writing in a specific format or style, or on a topic that the two of you have shared and enjoyed, using the published piece as a guide. For instance, a beginning writer might copy the pattern of Brian Wildsmith's *Cat on the Mat* (1983). A 7- or 8-year-old child might try writing a proverb in the style of Mem Fox's *Feathers and Fools* (2000). Your 13-year-old might try his hand at an opinion column based on George Will, or a humor column like Dave Barry's.

The following are some resources to help your child recognize and produce good writing:

- *After the End: Teaching and Learning Creative Revision* by Barry Lane, published in 1993. Lane helps you see that revision is actually an ongoing part of the creative process, *not* simply the act of cleaning up sloppy copy. It is full of solid ideas that can enhance your child's ownership of revision in the writing process and can help him see it as a good part of the writing process.

- *Craft Lessons: Teaching Writing K–6* by Ralph Fletcher and JoAnn Portalupi, published in 1998. This book is an excellent guide to giving children fresh challenges for their writing by treating them like real, published authors. The approach to looking at their writing as a craft is inspiring to children and their mentors. Each craft lesson includes a suggestion for a brief discussion, concrete minilessons that can be used in individual or small group settings, and a listing of books and other texts appropriate to use with the minilesson.

- *Creating Writers Through 6-Trait Writing Assessment and Instruction* (4th ed.) by Vicki Spandel, published in 2005.

While this book is academic in format, and suited for teachers who desire a great deal of structure in teaching writing, its focus is on the traits found in all good writing and offers clear examples helpful to a child observing and noticing these traits, as well as developing them.

- *Nonfiction Craft Lessons: Teaching Information Writing K–8* by JoAnn Portalupi and Ralph Fletcher, published in 2001. Divided into sections addressing the differences between emerging, competent, and fluent writers, this book contains craft lessons directed at the various informational writing genres. Every lesson features a discussion, how to teach it, and resource material to use in the lesson.

Introduce Your Child to Other Writers

Chapter 5 includes resources for locating annual conferences and seminars on children's literature or writing for young people. There are many of these held in cities across the United States and Canada. Well-known, published authors are featured speakers, presenters, and facilitators at these conferences, and generally speak about their writing processes—specifically about where their ideas came from, and especially about their revising and editing experiences. Learning how much pride is taken by published authors in fixing their own writing can be helpful and exciting for aspiring writers. Many published authors sponsor writing groups or writing workshops. Additionally, many authors have written articles and books that encourage revision, and if your child is enthusiastic about their books, they may be inspired by these authors' advice and instructional writing techniques. Table 7 provides a list of writers who may inspire your young writer.

Table 7
Good Writers Who Inspire Young Writers

- Rick Walton, for his playful use with language and hilarious rhyme.
- Debra Frasier, for her ability to bring a story to life with amazing cut-paper illustrations that help create insight fitting to her stories.
- Jon Scieszka, for his ability to use the "gross effect" to invite reluctant readers (and boys) to the joy of the written word.
- Beverly Cleary, for her ability to create characters and settings that all children can relate to.
- Lois Lowry, for her examples of writing seriously and humorously about real characters seeking personal truth and strength.
- Jerry Spinelli, for his wonderful use of imagery to which every reader connects.
- Katherine Hannigan, fairly new on the scene, for her ability to create characters that steal hearts and surely live right next door.
- Phyllis Reynolds Naylor, for her creation of books that make us roll on the floor in laughter, or cry our eyes out.
- J. K. Rowling, who needs no comment, but created worldwide, historic phenomena by capturing the reluctant readers of every age in every land and making them love an orphaned wizard named Harry.
- Cynthia Voight, for her ability to know what young people think and feel and write to those feelings.

Many authors discuss their writing processes, including revision, on their Web sites, and these can be found using Internet search engines such as Google. In addition, some videotaped interviews with authors are available at libraries, and contain discussions of how the writers fix their own work.

Some notable examples that children and young adults in my college courses have enjoyed are listed below.

- *Mem Fox,* videorecording, written, produced, and directed by Diane Kolyer, for Trumpet Club, 1992. Through sharing her writing process, Mem Fox convinces the audience that getting the words just right is worth it, because readers love well-written stories; they'll want to hear them again and again.

- *Eric Carle,* videorecording, directed by Rawn Fulton and produced by Searchlight Films for Philomel Books and Scholastic Inc., 1993. Besides demonstrating his unique artistic collage methods, Carle speaks about writing from his heart, and explains that children are the best writers because they also write from their hearts.

- *Good Conversation! A Talk With Katherine Paterson,* videorecording, by Tim Podell Productions, 1999. Paterson explains how she develops her characters and plots, and how she draws on her experiences and the people in her life for ideas about her stories. She also tells about researching settings and historical time periods to bring her stories to life.

- *Patricia Polacco, Dream Keeper,* videorecording, directed by Rawn Fulton and produced by Searchlight Films for Philomel Books, 1996. Polacco draws on family stories from her childhood and her progenitors. She explains how she develops her stories from thought processes to illustrations.

Inspire Your Child to Revise
Because He Wants to Make it Better

Revision seems like a difficult thing. Children do not naturally know what to do once they finish a draft of an idea. Sometimes it's hard for us to know what to suggest, as well.

But, we can gain a stronger sense of how writing grows if we are becoming writers ourselves and if we continue to grow in our understanding of what good writing looks like. Author Anne Lamott (1995) has said,

> I know some very great writers, writers you love who write beautifully and have made a great deal of money, and not one of them sits down routinely feeling wildly enthusiastic and confident. Not one of them writes elegant first drafts. All right, one of them does, but we do not like her very much. (p. 22)

Revising actually feels good to an experienced writer. It's also scary, because it involves expanding or clarifying ideas, discovering new connections, and deleting trivial or irrelevant information. Revising may mean reordering sections of writing that were difficult in the first place, condensing stories and descriptions, changing our voice, and gaining a clearer sense of who our audience is. It may include hacking out whole paragraphs, or even starting over. Revision is scary, but it also feels good when it comes from the heart of the writer who put the words on the paper in the first place.

Learning to revise is learning to care enough about our message or our audience to ask and then answer these questions (see Table 8): Is my purpose for writing this clear? Did I say what I wanted to say in a clear and interesting way? Is reading this information simple and engaging, or difficult and stressful? Does this writing reflect the truth as I see it? Does it flow, or if not, what is in the way?

Revision requires some mental distance between the draft and the revising. Reading aloud is critical, because the ability to hear text in your head is very rare. True revision requires multiple readings. It is adequate for a beginning writer to read a whole draft through once and make any changes that occur to him or

Table 8
Revising Questions
• Is my purpose clear?   • Did I say what I wanted, clearly and in an interesting way?   • Is this simple and engaging, or difficult and stressful, to read?   • Does this reflect truth as I see it?   • Does this flow, and if not, what is in the way?

her. But, as the writing maturity grows, the writer will actually become able to start reading the text at different points, through different eyes.

One of the most powerful lessons on the positive aspects of learning how to revise is to see a published author's drafts and revisions that preceded the published product. My son found the Web site of one of his favorite contemporary authors and wrote to him. The author wrote back through the regular mail, and sent him a page of a handwritten manuscript from the original draft of a published book. It is not unreasonable to request that of some authors. You never know what they would be willing to do as an example of their writing craft.

If your child is excited by the opportunity to publish, learning to revise will eventually come in a natural way. You can help by modeling the revision questions, but letting your child see the answers. Above all, honor content. After all, "Nobody buys books to marvel at the lovely sprinkling of commas and periods. But the presentation of wonderful ideas, well, that kind of book people will stand in line to buy" (Cramer, 2001, p. 109).

Do all you can to help your child view revision as a separate process from editing. *Revising* is changing how we think about our idea. *Editing* is cleaning it up in conventional ways so that others will *want* to read it.

The following are some resources to enhance the revision process:

- *After the End: Teaching and Learning Creative Revision* by Barry Lane, published in 1993. Lane helps you see that revision is actually an ongoing part of the creative process, not simply the act of cleaning up sloppy copy. It is full of solid ideas that can enhance your child's ownership of revision in the writing process.
- *Nonfiction Craft Lessons: Teaching Information Writing K–8* by JoAnn Portalupi and Ralph Fletcher, published in 2001. Divided into sections addressing the differences between emerging, competent, and fluent writers, this book contains craft lessons directed at the various informational writing genres. Every lesson features a discussion, how to teach it, and resource material to use in the lesson.
- *Reviser's Toolbox* by Barry Lane, published in 1999. Lane is also the author of *After the End*, annotated above. Based on those principles, *Reviser's Toolbox* is a practical self-selecting resource for the reading child to use on her own, or for the parent to work through with the child.

Keep Editing in an Appropriate Perspective

In *Creating Writers Through 6-Trait Writing Assessment and Instruction,* Vicki Spandel (2005b) says that conventions fall into two categories, textual and visual:

Textual conventions cover anything a copy editor would deal with: spelling, punctuation, grammar and usage, capitalization, and paragraphing . . . Such conventions clearly change over time, and so to assess or teach them well, we need to rely on up-to-date handbooks and dictionaries and use them often. Textual conventions not only support meaning but also help readers to understand intended inflection and voice . . . Visual conventions (also known as presentation) are so called because they visually organize text, guiding the reader's eye and making certain points stand out. They include such things as graphics (maps, charts, photographs) that support text or expand meaning, use of bulleted or numbered lists, and use of titles and subheads. Visual conventions are more important in some kinds of text than in others . . . , and you should respond to them accordingly. They need not be considered for every paper. (p. 121)

With our support, children can come to think of editing as a courtesy to help readers feel at home. Most editing occurs after a draft is finished, and it helps us ensure that the conventions of writing we have used support the meaning we want our writing to have. The best and least intrusive way to develop a desire and skill for editing requires a few steps, including:

- use excellent and current handbooks,
- use available tools that include dictionaries and computer spell-checker programs,
- ask for help from qualified editors,
- read drafts both silently and aloud to check for visual and audible errors,
- gain some mental distance by leaving the draft alone for a time prior to editing, and
- leave wide margins and double spaces on the draft to allow room for corrections.

One of the most effective influences you can have on your child's writing is to give the red pen to her. Professional writers develop their own editing skills out of a pride in turning in work that their editors will want to read. It is often difficult for us as parents to allow our children to learn and work through editing processes, especially if we were corrected by adults when we were learning to write. You may actually feel guilty, thinking that you cannot possibly benefit from your allowing all of those errors to slip away. Besides, when *you* do the editing, it may feel like you are *doing* a lot. You *are*, but there is absolutely no research to indicate that children learn from corrections to their writing made by adults. They *do* learn when adults define and model appropriate use of conventions, when adults offer frequent guided practice with the child doing the editing on her own text. Spandel (2005b) compares adult editing of children's writing to teaching multiplication of fractions. "If one of your students got 10 or 20 problems wrong, would you provide additional instruction and practice—or would you simply do the problems *for* the student so that he could copy the correct answers?" (p. 202).

> One of the most effective influences you can have on your child's writing is to give the red pen to her. Professional writers develop their own editing skills out of a pride in turning in work that their editors will want to read.

As with the motivation to revise, the most powerful motivation for editing is helping create in the child a desire to publish the writing for a particular audience, or to want someone to want to read it. Children can learn to care about what others think about their writing. They are usually amazed to learn that real companies who publish books *pay* people to edit. If the reading audience were to find misspellings, poor grammar, and no punctuation, they would not want to buy the book and would not want to read what we write.

The following resources can be used to teach your child writing conventions and editing skills:

- *Barron's Pocket Guide to Correct Grammar* by Vincent Hopper and others, published in 2004. This is a newer edition with an attractive design and easy-to-find information on grammar usage.

- *The Elements of Style* (4th ed.) by William Strunk, Jr., E. B. White, and Roger Angell, published in 2000. This book is timeless; English teachers and their students have used this compact book since it was first published in 1957.
- *Langenscheidt's Pocket Guide to Punctuation and Style* by Langenscheidt staff, published in 2000. This book is modern, and contains internationally universal thought on style and punctuation.
- *A Pocket Guide to Correct Punctuation* (4th ed.) by Robert Brittain and Benjamin W. Griffith, published in 1997. This small book is a helpful guide to correct punctuation, with explanations of the conventions.
- *Write On: A Conference Approach to Writing* by Jo-Ann Parry and David Hornsby, published in 1985. There are numerous used copies of this older book that can be found and purchased very inexpensively on book Web sites and in used bookstores. Its chapters are short and concise, and offer excellent suggestions for the entire writing process, but especially for addressing the development of skills in spelling, grammar, and usage within the context of the writing process.
- *Write Right!: A Desktop Digest of Punctuation, Grammar, and Style* by Jan Venolia, published in 2001. This is a useful and reliable writing guide that covers the essentials of good writing in a concise and easy-to-follow format.

Give Your Child Time to Write

Set things up so that your child has every possible opportunity to see herself as a writer. Having time is critical to meaningful, purposeful writing. While time for writing within many school classrooms has increased in recent years, it is far short of what is needed to promote successful writers. Writing requires some consistency and some continuity. Engaged writers need time to enter into what Donald Graves (1994) calls "a constant state of composition" (p. 104). This is where the writer rehearses what he will say, or runs the text through his head. The writing process for anyone takes time, and your gifted writer deserves to have the luxury of enough time for his process to be honored and inspired.

By empowering your child to take charge of her own writing process, to know and act upon the difference between strong and weak writing, and to revise and edit her own work because of her own desire to do so, you will be empowering your child and encouraging her success. Many potential writers have never experienced the joy of that moment when they hear their own voice or see how much their writing has touched someone. You can empower you child to open her heart and yours.

Giving Gifted Writers What They Need

The following list is included to help you develop the surroundings, circumstances, attitudes, resources, and mentorship your gifted writer needs and deserves. This list can also be used as a checklist with which you may assess a school's writing program or any other program you may find to assist you in your goals. Gifted writers need:

- *inspiration* to expand thinking and develop their ideas;
- *multiple and varied life experiences* to which they can refer while composing;
- *opportunities to enjoy, explore, and experiment* with words and language;

- *time* (a good portion of it, unhurried) to write;
- *space* that is personalized, inspirational, and with some degree of ownership;
- *quality materials*—all artists, scientists, or practitioners in any field thrive when they have access to the best tools of the best quality;
- easy access to a *wide and large variety of reference books and materials*, such as dictionaries, thesauruses, and language arts picture books;
- *passionate mentoring* (as opposed to assignments, drills, and repetitious, boring practices) or the child's sure knowledge that someone who knows about or is good at writing, knows about and appreciates the child's writing;
- *recognition and appreciation for originality and diversity*; and
- *safe environments for taking risks*, free from unexpected and unsolicited criticism.

There is a tendency among inexperienced or misguided teachers to skip the first step—inspiration—and cut writing down to the basics. However, careful thought and your best creative efforts should be given to this as the first and most important first step. Quality of every other step will follow when you begin with wonderful words and fantastic forms of inspiration. Inspiration runs the gamut all the way from reading aloud a delightful book, asking intriguing questions, and posing "what if" scenarios, all the way to visiting newspaper offices, libraries, bookstores, publishing companies, printing presses, advertising offices, television stations where the stories are written, authors' homes, or writing conferences.

Each element of the list above is imperative for serious and able writers. Young gifted writers *deserve* these things because they deserve opportunities to pursue advanced work at an accelerated pace. They will be empowered to investigate topics of interest in depth (an opportunity they seldom receive in regular school classrooms). They will be able to explore a broad range of writing genres, while still having their favorite authors, genres, and specific titles. They will not only be required to apply a host of practical research skills, but they will *want* to do so. In fact, they will likely feel thrilled by their research endeavors. Many gifted writers who receive what they need as writers exhibit greater than average flexibility in their attempts at more difficult kinds of writing (poetry, drama, short fiction pieces). They usually exhibit greater flexibility in the use of materials, time, and resources.

Serious and passionate writers who are affirmed by receiving what they need will show increasingly higher expectations for personal independence and persistence to their writing tasks. They love (and need) discussion opportunities about their writing in order to interpret the opinions and feelings of others about their work.

The final item in this list of what gifted writers need and deserve is perhaps predictable. But, I hope my emphasis is not so predictable, because this need must be addressed appropriately in order not to undo everything you have wanted and desired for your gifted writer. Your child deserves learning based on her needs, almost as they arise, rather than in a predetermined order or sequence of instruction. Teachers in classrooms may indeed control what is *taught,* but each individual child in that classroom controls what is *learned.* You can teach effectively and your child can learn successfully, if you can strive for an on demand or as needed system for presenting the conventions and skills your child deserves and wants. See the resource list in Chapter 5 for ways to address these matters.

Some of the titles I have listed in Chapter 5 target classroom teachers, and may be the means of your developing a rapport with your child's teacher in cosupporting the writing workshop or other programs that will help your child develop his or her full writing potential. You may also find them helpful in developing your own philosophy about writing, and in providing for your child's needs on your own.

A Word About Very Young Children Writing

Every word that a child sets to paper should be celebrated. At first, her words will be in the form of letters and combinations of letters that represent the sounds the child intends, even if the conventional words are not all present yet. The focus of encouragement and mentoring for young children takes the shape of talking, interactively writing words on paper (taking turns on the same paper, or papers side by side), or asking each other to read back what you've written or what the child thinks she has written. Young children are inspired to take the risks involved in communicating when they care about what they write, and when they believe you care. Figure 9 is a 4-year-old child's description of a sad event that she witnessed. A special note: Voluntary illustration makes the writing process for very young children extremely enjoyable for your child and for you.

Children are often willing to give writing a try when they feel strong emotion about something. For many children, it is almost like unlocking the feelings that are just waiting to escape. Figure 10 shows how a 5-year-old felt about being at school when he would rather have been at home. He had been crying since he was left at school an hour before his writing time.

Notice in Figures 9 and 10 that the children have written on unlined paper, and one of them created his own lines to support his message. Emerging writers can be encouraged to do this as a

"My ducks ate my fish."

Figure 9. A young child's drawing and writing

step toward planning what they want to say and feeling supported in writing it. They first decide what they want to say. Then they count the words and sounds they think they will use, and write out a number of support lines onto which they will write their words.

Revision with young children should be only very minimal at first. Asking them to read to you what they have written, and letting them know what more you would like to know about

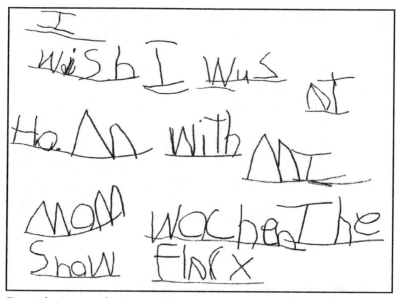

"I wish I was home with my mom, watching the snow flakes."

Figure 10. A young child's thoughts

it should be the extent of your revision requirements. As they gain more experience and confidence, you can begin to introduce the revision questions one at a time over a long period of time. Editing must be more delicate because demanding multiple conventions of a young child before he has any understanding of what most of them represent may stifle the natural course of development of conventional knowledge that is desired. A premature push for correct spelling and complicated punctuation can dash the beginning instincts of a young writer.

When you find it appropriate to teach specific conventions, introducing them in fun and enjoyable ways will be more effective than defining and drilling your child on what they are and how they should be used. Some clever authors have presented a variety of conventions in great read-aloud and picture book formats. Some annotated examples follow:

- Brian P. Cleary's books *Hairy, Scary, Ordinary: What Is an Adjective* (2001); *I and You and Don't Forget Who: What Is a Pronoun?* (2004); *A Mink, a Fink, a Skating Rink: What Is a Noun?* (1999); and *To Root, to Toot, to Parachute: What Is a Verb?* (2001) are lively and worthy of multiple reads.

- Ruth Heller's books *Many Luscious Lollipops: A Book About Adjectives* (1998); *Mine, All Mine: A Book About Pronouns* (2001); *Merry-Go-Round: A Book About Nouns* (1998); *Behind the Mask: A Book About Prepositions* (1998); and *Fantastic! Wow! and Unreal!: A Book About Interjections and Conjunctions* (2000) all are gloriously illustrated and poetically presented to make each convention addressed clearly understandable.

- Robin Pulver's *Punctuation Takes a Vacation* (2003), features punctuation marks as the main characters in this story, and the plot helps them explain themselves and their importance.

- Marvin Terban's books *Your Foot's on My Feet and Other Tricky Nouns* (1986); *The Dove Dove: Funny Homograph Riddles* (1988); *Eight Ate: A Feast of Homonym Riddles* (1982); *Too Hot to Hoot: Funny Palindrome Riddles* (1985); and *Mad as a Wet Hen! And Other Funny Idioms* (1987) are fun to share with a child as you attempt to outguess each other on correct answers to riddles about these tricky subjects. Each convention is explained and discussed in the front of the book.

- Peggy Parish's *Amelia Bedelia* series are delightful books that utilize idioms and figurative language.

- Rick Walton's *Once There Was a Bull . . . frog* (1997); *Bullfrog Pops!* (1999); *Herd of Cows! Flock of Sheep!* (2002); *Why the Banana Split* (1998); *Pig Pigger Piggest* (2003); and *Suddenly*

Alligator: An Adverbial Tale (2001) are all picture books that address different parts of speech from adverbs, to collective nouns, to comparative adjectives in fun stories.

Children learn about good writing from good experiences with reading and stimulating opportunities to write. Chapter 2 contains a section entitled Make a Mark, Leave a Record, Tell a Story. These ideas are suggested for increasing a family enjoyment for interaction in writing activities. These enjoyable activities will encourage writing talk, writing drafts, and many writing products. Our children will learn to find satisfaction in the hard work of revisions when revision means they have discovered ideas and solved the problems of print. Children learn to use punctuation, grammar, and spelling effectively when they are able to laugh along with authors and illustrators as they come to love the conventions of print.

Chapter 5

Enrichment Resources for Your Young Writer

In the best writing—writing that makes you want to grab whoever's nearby and say, "Here, read this!"— the trails lead to unexpected and delightful places.
—*Stephen Kramer, 2005*

R egardless of how much of the support you provide for your young writer, the simple fact is that you cannot do it *all* alone. By making these decisions about how best to encourage your child's writing ability and achievement, you are positively and proactively affecting his future. Most of the potential outcomes will not be measurable until he is an adult. One way to enhance your child's potential is through enrichment opportunities outside of school and home. There are numerous resources, organizations, and caring people who can help you and improve the experience for you and your child. They can benefit your child by affirming his ability and by reinforcing what you believe about your child. Involvement in outside enrichment opportunities can also serve as your training for future support efforts that you can offer.

This annotated list of resources is meant for your personalization, according to what you and your child have determined your needs and interests to be. If something sounds good to you, look it up on the Internet or at your local library and scan the book or the site for yourself. When looking at schools, workshops, and other programs, procure recommendations and assessment documents that will help you determine the program's suitability to your circumstance. This list, while comprehensive, is not complete. These are, however, respectable sources of high quality.

Additional Books to Guide Your Child

- *Awakening the Heart: Exploring Poetry in Elementary and Middle School* (1999) by Georgia Heard. Poetry can be the perfect place to start with some children, because of assured success for delighting the writer and the reader early on in the process. Georgia Heard knows the hearts of poets, especially child poets.
- *Craft Lessons: Teaching Writing K–8* (1998) by Ralph Fletcher and JoAnn Portalupi. I have referred to this book and its companion book, *Nonfiction Craft Lessons: Teaching Information Writing K–8* (2001) in previous chapters. It is truly a well-kept secret as far as its applicability to parents working with their children as writers.
- *Families Writing* (1998) by Peter R. Stillman. This wonderful little paperback is out of print, but if you can find it at a used bookstore or from your favorite Internet source for used books, it will likely be worth the time and trouble. He wrote this book to encourage families to maintain close-knit ties.

- *Getting Kids Published: A Practical Guide for Helping Young Authors See Their Works in Print* (1994) by Jamie Whitfield. Because it can be difficult to find opportunities to put young authors' work into print, this guidebook offers teachers practical information for finding authentic audiences for their students' writing. The information ranges from discussions of prewriting ideas to techniques for encouraging cooperative editing. It's a great resource.
- *If You Can Talk, You Can Write* (1993) by Joel Saltzman. This book is not for children, but its premise will inspire you to become a writer, and give you ideas for mentoring your child as a writer. The book is based on Saltzman's successful writing seminars by the same name, and his main point is that writing does not have to be intimidating if we remember that it is a form of communication, much like talking.
- *If You're Trying to Teach Kids How to Write, You've Gotta Have this Book!* (1995) by Marjorie Frank. This book contains fresh ideas and good-sense advice. It's a classic resource for teachers and will go a long way toward inspiring you to inspire your child, as well.
- *The Living Classroom: Writing, Reading, and Beyond* (1997) by David Armington. This book is about one teacher's respect for children's ideas and their work as outward and visible signs of their thinking. The teacher, Ms. Amidon, pays passionate attention to her students, and is a wonderful and vivid example of "living" within a classroom community. The ideas exemplified in this book are powerful inspirations for parents of writing children.
- *The Magic Pencil: Teaching Children Creative Writing* (1988) by Eve Shelnutt. This simple resource is thorough without overwhelming the reader. It includes excellent information about what to do when children make errors, and exercises

to motivate young writers (even the reluctant ones). Each chapter or lesson explains the age or grade level that would be appropriate, a list of concepts that are being taught, and clear, brief explanations about what to do.

- *On Writing Well* (2001) by William Zinsser. Recently released in a special 25th anniversary edition, this book, used widely by writers and students of nonfiction, is the ultimate guide for science and technical writing, business writing, sports, and humor. Easily understood by adolescents who are serious about themselves as writers, this book has helpful suggestions for any writer; simplicity is the key, strength and clarity is imperative, and all writers should read their work aloud to make sure what they write is actually something they would say. If your child ends up studying writing or journalism in college, his professors are sure to be impressed if he is already very familiar with Zinsser's book.

- *Sharing the Pen: Interactive Writing With Young Children* (2004) by Gail E. Tompkins and Stephanie Collom. Interactive writing is the bridge between adult-directed writing and independent writing by the child. It is a strategy most commonly used with emergent and early writers, as well as struggling older writers. Its implementation is empowering, and this book can not only help teachers (and parents) understand how to engage in it, but a thorough understanding of its theoretical underpinnings is also clearly presented.

- *Teaching Poetry: Yes You Can!* (1993) by Jacqueline Sweeney. Practical and lively ways to engage your child in a variety of poetry experiences are contained in this book, along with poems by famous authors as inspiration.

- *What a Writer Needs* (1993) by Ralph Fletcher. In this book's forward, Donald M. Murray says that he has not read another book that does what this book does; it speaks to the heart of anyone who wishes to mentor a young writer. Fletcher provides a wealth of specific, practical strategies for inspiring students' writing.

- *Word Weavings: Writing Poetry With Young Children* (1997) by Shelley Tucker. If poetry seems like a great place to start— one that will motivate both you and your child (grades K–2), either this book, or its companion for grades 3–6, *Painting the Sky: Writing Poetry With Children* (1995), is an excellent choice. These books include inspiring examples, lots of motivation, and exciting ways to produce all types of poetry.
- *The Writer's Path: A Guidebook for Your Creative Journey* (2000) by Todd Walton and Mindy Toomay. In this book you will find a wide variety of writing exercises that are fun, easy, and inviting for both you and your child.
- *Writing Toward Home: Tales and Lessons to Find Your Way* (1995) by Georgia Heard. This book was extremely inspiring to me, and you may find it the same. The narratives and suggested exercises can be modified for younger children, or used as is for older children. You will want to keep (or provide your child with) a writer's notebook.
- *Written & Illustrated By . . . : A Revolutionary Two-Brain Approach for Teaching Students How to Write and Illustrate Amazing Books* (1985) by David Melton. This book is well-suited for use as a text or guideline for writing and creating books with children of any age. It works well in a group setting, or with individual children, and informs them of the complete process of writing a book.

Books Your Child Will Want to Read

Some children are ready to take on the biggest portion of the responsibility for their growth as writers. The following books are written with the purpose of inspiring budding and blossoming young writers. They are fairly inexpensive, and worth the investment, as well as the time to share them with your child.

- *How Writers Work: Finding a Process That Works for You* (2000) by Ralph Fletcher. A small, inexpensive paperback, written to the child, this describes how writers work and how your child can make words do what he intends for them to do. This is an empowering guide to young writers, who will find the inspiration to take their writing seriously, while having a great time.

- *Live Writing: Breathing Life Into Your Words* (1999) by Ralph Fletcher. This small paperback is written to the child to give him or her some practical strategies to add to his or her writer's toolbox. Fletcher introduces writers to tools to make words jump right off the page and into the heart of the reader.

- *Market Guide for Young Writers: Where and How to Sell What You Write* (1996) by Kathy Henderson. This book is a great tool for encouraging students to enter their writing in contests and for publication. The science of submission is clearly outlined, as well as how to prepare a manuscript.

- *Poetry Matters: Writing a Poem From the Inside Out* (2002) by Ralph Fletcher. This small, inexpensive paperback is written to the child, and also makes a great read-aloud. It is about writing poetry, not analyzing it, and Fletcher's purpose in writing it was his desire for children to have "wonderful moments" with poetry, and to feel its power. They will with this book.

- *Reviser's Toolbox* (1999) by Barry Lane. *Reviser's Toolbox* is a practical, self-selecting resource for the reading child to use on her own, or for the parent to work through with the child. The chapters can be skimmed for what is most applicable to the child's work or used for specific concept development in improving writing. One of the most valuable parts of this book is the teaching bibliography included in the appendix. By category, Lane lists great models for writing and using literary devices.

- *Write Where You Are: How to Use Writing to Make Sense of Your Life: A Guide For Teens* (1999) by Caryn Mirriam-Goldberg. This creative writing guide also serves as a self-help book for teens, with writing exercises designed to get young people to know and like themselves while learning the craft of writing. Its conversational tone is inspiring for teens who are interested in writing and willing (or even reluctant) to give it a try.

- *A Writer's Notebook: Unlocking the Writer Within You* (1996) by Ralph Fletcher. This small, inexpensive paperback written to the child who wants to be a writer describes how writers use notebooks as records of their dreams, feelings, thoughts, and observations. This book is enjoyable when read aloud to your family, or just between you and your child. Your child will want a journal (maybe more than one) to get started right away.

- *Writing With Authors Kids Love! Writing Exercises by Authors of Children's Literature* (1998) edited by Kathryn Lee Johnson. This compilation of writing exercises developed by children's literature authors offers students creative ideas that make their writing fun and meaningful. You can certainly use the book as a parent to teach the lessons. However, there is value in letting these authors speak directly to your child, when you locate and share the specific works listed in this collection.

The Publishing World and Children

Happy is he who . . . writes from the love of imparting certain thoughts and not from the necessity of sale—who writes always to *the unknown friend.*

—Ralph Waldo Emerson, April 1845

Because publishing experiences are powerful motivators to children to do the intense work of drafting ideas, revising messages, and fixing the conventional problems in their writing, unique and innovative ideas for publishing are a must. Our first thoughts are likely to lead us to seek legitimate publishing sources for our children to work for. Finding a publishing home for a manuscript is a challenge and a difficult task for many adult would-be writers. It will be even more difficult for children, unless you are able to work with a company that specifically publishes children's work. There is a handful of magazine and book publishing companies that do accept admissions from children.

We must be sure to not be the pushers and enforcers of our children's submission processes. We can certainly help our children in the pursuits of being real authors by supporting, mentoring, inspiring, and providing a nurturing environment, as described in previous chapters. We can gently guide them through the journey of preparing themselves and their writing for the publishing world at the appropriate time and place for them.

Preparing a manuscript for submission to an editor who will give it serious consideration is a complicated and exacting task, even if the manuscript itself is worthy, by regular standards, of being published. Young children may be distracted from their development of sincere and authentic writing ability if they are prematurely encouraged to attempt to be published. Many high school aged children *are* ready to investigate and navigate through the publishing world. Becoming profitably published is difficult. Extremely difficult. It is not a commonly appropriate goal for young children to be published in comparable ways, but it may be entirely appropriate for some of our young writers to get a head start on this very gratifying, but humbling task.

Everyone interested in writing *for* children should avail themselves of a copy of *Children's Writer's & Illustrator's Market,* published by Writers Digest Books, and updated yearly. *Children's Writer's & Illustrator's Market* provides information about book publishers, magazines, agents, contact names, submission guidelines, pay rates, Web sites, e-mail addresses, and phone numbers. There are clear and effective guidelines for writing effective query letters, preparing professional submissions, and information about organizations, conferences, and contests. Between 300 and 400 pages are filled each year with the most current information for those on the path to publication. If you and your child choose to begin a submission process for his or her writing, use this guide as a resource and follow the guidelines and suggestions within.

In addition, several print and online magazines publish children's creative work. Listed below is contact and publication information for several of these publishing outlets.

Magazines That Publish Children's Work

- *Creative Kids: The National Voice for Kids.* This interactive magazine by and for kids ages 8–14 is a Parents' Choice award-winning publication. Besides stimulating activities such as brain teasers, contests, and pen pals, *Creative Kids* magazine includes prose, poetry, games, artwork, and opinion pieces. *Creative Kids* boasts student submissions from all over the world. For subscription information and to download sample articles, visit http://www.prufrock.com, write to Prufrock Press Inc., P.O. Box 8813, Waco, TX 76714-8813, or call (800) 998-2208.

- *Stone Soup.* This beautiful magazine by young writers and artists includes stories, poetry, and art from children all over the world. The Web site (http://www.stonesoup.com) is as valuable as the magazine itself. The Web site includes a sample issue to read, a secure order form, and recordings of child authors reading their own work. The site also provides links to resources such as other print magazines for young writers, children's museums around the world, finding a pen pal, and supporting children in conflict around the world. To subscribe, you can call toll free from the U.S. and Canada (800) 447-4569 or write to Stone Soup Subscriptions Department, P.O. Box 83, Santa Cruz, CA 95063.

- *Merlyn's Pen.* This magazine showcases compelling works of fiction and nonfiction authored by American teens in grades 6–12. The magazine recently began a new monthly edition that can be found on the Web and printed from the web. Access *Merlyn's* Pen at http://www.merlynspen.org/magazine.

- *New Moon.* This magazine is edited by and for girls ages 8–14. It includes fiction, poetry, artwork, and letters, as well as learning activities and curricula. The articles describe the lives of girls and women around the globe. *New Moon* has received six Parents Choice awards. Visit http://www.newmoon.org or write to *New Moon*, 2 West First Street #101, Duluth, MN 55802.

- *Potluck Magazine.* The mission of this magazine is to provide an educational and professional forum to encourage young writers ages 8–16, although they have published work from children as young as 4. They receive more than 600 submissions of poetry, stories, fables, book reviews, and artwork for each edition, and their editors read and respond to each one. Writers or artists who are not published in *Potluck Magazine* receive personal letters along with a constructive and positive critique of their work. For more information and to subscribe, visit the Web site at http://www.potluckmagazine.org or write to *Potluck Magazine,* Box 546, Deerfield, IL 60015.
- *Skipping Stones.* This is an award-winning children's magazine that encourages cooperation, creativity, and celebration of cultural and environmental richness. It is published bimonthly during the school year, and accepts art and original writings in every language and from all ages. Previous issues include stories, articles, and photos from all over the world, including Native American folktales, photos taken by kids in India and the Ukraine, letters and drawings from South Africa and Lithuania, and cartoons from China. Non-English writings are accompanied by English translations to encourage the learning of other languages. Each issue also contains international pen pals, book reviews, news, and a guide for parents and teachers for using *Skipping Stones* in the home or classroom. Visit http://www.skippingstones. org or write to *Skipping Stones Magazine,* P.O. Box 3939, Eugene, OR 97403-0939.

Web Sites That Publish Children's Work

- *KidPub Children's Publishing:* http://www.kidpub.org/kidpub. This site offers features that entice a young budding author to submit writing for a more public audience than she has at home or school. Participation on the site requires registration of a user name and password. The features include an Author's Forum, where children can suggest story ideas and talk about writing. KidPub Publisher's Picks is a section that posts the publisher's favorite stories and poems. There also is a Question and Answers section and a never-ending story to which children may add their contributions.

- *International Kids' Space*: http://www.kids-space.org. This pleasant format invites children to post their writing, and allows children to read other children's writing from all around the world. Submissions are organized by date and subject.

- *MidLink Magazine*: http://longwood.cs.ucf.edu/~MidLink. This digital magazine for middle grade and high school kids, was created by kids for kids. It includes submissions from children all over the world.

- *Potato Hill Poetry*: http://www.potatohill.com. This Web site dedicates itself to igniting a passion for poetry in schools throughout the United States. Besides posting poetry from children and adults, it includes writing exercises, teaching resources, and writing contest information.

- *The Writers' Slate*: http://www.writingconference.com/writers.htm. Originally a print magazine, this publication is now online, and accepts original poetry and prose from students in grades K–12. One of its three issues each year is devoted to publishing winners of the writing contests sponsored by the magazine. You can send manuscripts to 7619 Hemlock Street, Overland Park, KS 66204.

- *Young Writers Club*: http://www.cs.bilkent.edu.tr/~david/derya/ywc.html. This club aims to encourage children to enjoy writing by encouraging them to share their work and help each other improve their writing abilities. The club posts submission criteria based on current needs, such as a request for well-written nonfiction articles.

- *Young Writers' Clubhouse*: http://www.realkids.com/club.shtml. At this site, children can learn about different aspects of the writing process. Young writers are encouraged to share stories and poems they have written themselves and seek constructive feedback from other child writers.

Making Books to Inspire Writers

The following resources can inspire your child to publish and create books for friends and family members. These books treat children's self-publishing as an art that they can come to love. The book-making ideas range from creative but simple reuses of discarded items, to instructions for a variety of historic and temporary artistic book formats. An additional bonus of these books is how they will likely enthuse you and your child to enjoy a new hobby together.

- *Cover to Cover: Creative Techniques for Making Beautiful Books, Journals, & Albums* (2000) by Shereen LaPlantz. This colorfully photographed and illustrated book gives step-by-step directions for making the books that are beautifully depicted on its pages. Tools, techniques, and parts of books are all explained visually and clearly.
- *In Print! 40 Cool Publishing Projects for Kids* (2003) by Joe Rhatigan. This colorfully photographed book will inspire you to create publishing projects that look great and are worthy of great writing. You and your child will want your words to live long after you're gone, and this book prompts you to cherish your child's writing for a lifetime. Projects are unique

and fascinating, and include everything from cement stepping-stones with writing on them for the garden, to maze books stored in a handmade box. Sprinkled throughout the pages of this book are little instructions for a variety of brainstorming techniques.

- *Making Books That Fly, Fold, Wrap, Hide, Pop Up, Twist, and Turn* (1998), by Gwen Diehn. This book is designed to help you and your child make books, as well as to think of topics to make your books about. Again, these colorful illustrations and photographs will inspire book projects that carry messages across space and time, books that celebrate things, and books that help us make sense of experiences. This book will help you create treasures to keep.

Themed Literature Inspiration

You may have a natural sense for building a meaningful curriculum or program that suits your child and you better than programs included in books, on Web sites, or in schools. It may be that the only support you need is a list of fresh ideas and suggestions for unique writing opportunities that you can tailor to fit your child and your circumstances. A few themed literature investigations were introduced in Chapter 1 (teddy bears, baseball, and Cinderella), but the ideas are limitless. Draw on the interests you know your child has or that you share with him. Draw on the expertise of those close to you. And, when you have exhausted all of those ideas (in truth, you are not likely to exhaust them before your child grows up and leaves home), start through an old set of encyclopedias, if you can find one. You and your child might set out to update a volume or two of this antiquated resource with original compositions based on your own dynamic explorations, investigations, and experiences. The magic of this option is that you are complete control of the structures, the inspiration, and the outcomes.

Schools/Classes/Workshops

Schools are ideal options for some families because they offer a respectable trail of experience and documented quality, provide publicly-stated philosophies, and have usually earned some type of accreditation that assures quality in this school. Be certain to verify this accreditation before committing to fees and attendance. Credible writing schools and programs will be widely documented, and you will be given sources from which you can seek recommendations and feedback from others who have utilized the program. Check with your school district to see if course credit can be transferred from the special course to your child's secondary transcript. The ability to earn credit toward graduation may be important to your decision, but it should not be the only consideration. One important element in the decision to enroll your child in a school is to not give your child the impression that you want to pass along his writing aspirations to someone else's care. Your child needs to feel a strong sense of your caring enough to find just the right match for your child's unique and individual needs.

Classes are ideal for families just beginning the journey of nurturing a writer, because they are short-termed and usually require moderate fees, so that you won't feel you are investing blindly in your child's future. Workshops provide the same benefit, and the costs are usually very affordable. You can likely trust the age and grade level information offered by each program, because if they have been in business for a while, they have determined appropriate ages for their programs. Instruction in schools and summer programs is very often accelerated, so you can be assured that your child is being challenged at the level he belongs. The following resources were current offerings at the time of this writing.

Programs Throughout the Year

- *Belin-Blank Center at the University of Iowa*: http://www. education.uiowa.edu/belinblank. This center offers academic year "challenge Saturday" programs, as well as summer institutes and talent search programs.
- *Center for Talented Youth (CTY) at Johns Hopkins University*: http://www.jhu.edu/~gifted. CTY offers fall enrollment, and this talent search is open to students in grades 2–8. This program allows you to learn more about your child's math and verbal reasoning abilities, and support you in ways to recognize those advanced abilities, including family academic conferences, hosted at various locations around the country.
- *College for Kids at the University of Wisconsin, Madison*: http://www.soemadison.wisc.edu/cfk. The University of Wisconsin at Madison offers education outreach youth programs designed to provide a quality precollege learning experience. Young students come to the campus where children's respect for originality, openness to new perspectives, new academic areas, and innovative career choices are promoted. There is summer and year-round programming for experiences not found in the regular classroom. Children have access to state-of-the-art resources and highly skilled instructors. Partnerships and collaborations are developed with many school districts, community centers, and commu-

nity organizations. Updates, registration, and resources are available on the Web site.

- *Duke TIP Summer Studies Programs*: http://www.tip. duke.edu/summer_programs. These programs offer students in grades 7–10 the opportunity to learn highly challenging material at a rate suited to their advanced abilities. Students enroll in a single Duke TIP-designed course for 3 weeks of in-depth study; they attend nearly 40 hours of class each week between Monday morning and Saturday afternoon. Programs are offered on a variety of college campuses, providing opportunities for students to experience college classroom instruction and residence hall living. Classes have approximately 16 students and are taught by highly qualified teaching teams. Outside the classroom, a carefully selected residential staff supervises students during meals, free time, and social and recreational activities. One writing program is called "A Writer's Art: Creative Writing," and takes 10th to 12th grade students to Ghost Ranch, NM.

- *Duke TIP's e-Studies Program*: http://www.tip.duke.edu/ e-studies. This is a distance-learning opportunity that connects students with other gifted students and with a TIP instructor as they pursue advanced high school and college-level coursework on the Internet.

- *Duke University TIP Academic Adventures Program*: http:// www.tip.duke.edu/academic_year_programs/academic_ adventures. This program is designed as a benefit for students participating in the Duke University TIP Talent Search, where students attend day-long Saturday programs, choosing from array of exciting classes to pursue a topic in depth. An optional parent session is offered in conjunction with the Saturday program.

- *Duke University TIP Scholar Weekends*: http://www.tip.duke. edu/academic_year_programs/scholar_weekends. These weekend programs are designed for students in grades 8–12 (depending on site) to take short courses that introduce topics that might not be available in local schools. They provide enrichment, a glimpse into the collegiate experience, and an opportunity to meet other similarly motivated students.
- *Gotham Writers' Workshop*: http://www.writingclasses.com. This program claims the distinction of being the largest and most comprehensive private creative writing school in New York City and online. Ten-week and one-day workshops are offered in more than a dozen forms of writing including fiction writing, screenwriting, nonfiction writing, and more. The school also offers private instruction, script and book doctoring services, workshops for teens, and custom workshops for corporations. It was founded in New York City in 1993 by two creative writing graduates and former teachers of writing at a variety of schools and universities. The site boasts that half of all of the school's students enroll in online workshops, with many of its students living abroad, making these classes a global experience.
- *Institute for Educational Advancement*: http://www. educationaladvancement.org/resources/search/programs. php. This site allows you to fill in and select information in a search engine, and then produces a list of opportunities in a variety of academic and talent areas.
- *Johns Hopkins University Center for Talented Youth (CTY) Distance Education*: http://cty.jhu.edu/cde. This program provides challenging academic courses all year long for eligible students in grades K–12. The long-distance courses are varied, and writing course titles include "Writing for an Audience," "Crafting the Essay," "Writing Analysis and

Persuasion," "Crafting Poetry," and "Language Rules: From Structure to Style." The courses are demanding and very appropriate for highly able students, and students can take courses all year long, making significant progress in a subject by working from their homes or schools.

Summer Programs

- *Duke University's Talent Identification Program (Duke TIP)*: http://www.tip.duke.edu. Duke's TIP program identifies gifted children and provides resources to nurture their abilities, including the opportunity to learn more about their gifts.
- *Hoagies' Gifted Education Page*: http://www.hoagiesgifted. org/summer.htm. This site is a clearinghouse for a variety of gifted and talented summer programs. Most are held at colleges and universities and offer classes in many subject areas, including writing. This comprehensive list is worth looking at to determine if a talent search program will meet your family's situation, as well as your child's needs as a writer.
- *Johns Hopkins University Center for Talented Youth Summer Programs*: http://cty.jhu.edu/summer. CTY summer programs are offered at colleges and universities throughout the nation. The programs are 3 weeks long, and students take only one course. There is a residential program, where students live on campus under the supervision of resident assistants and participate in activities ranging from sports, to arts and crafts, to music and special events such as dances and a student talent show. There are also day programs where students come to campus each day for the duration of the program. Some writing courses include "Writing and Imagination" and "Writing Workshop: Where Art Meets Science."

- *National Association for Gifted Children*: http://www.nagc. org. This site offers information on how to choose a summer program for your child and lists camps according to state and areas of the country.
- *Stetson University HATS (High Achieving Talented Students) Summer Programs*: http://stetson.edu/hats/summer-programs. html. These programs occur throughout the state of Florida, in a variety of academic areas, including writing.
- *Summer Camps and Programs in New York State*: http://summer oncampus.com/main/ActivityList.asp. This site includes links to program information in all academic and other topic areas. The Journalism/Writing link includes a comprehensive list of a variety of programs, with contact information.
- *Summer Institute for the Gifted (SIG)*: http://giftedstudy. com. Academic summer camps for grades K–11 (both residential and day programs) are held at prestigious institutions of higher learning across the United States (Amherst College, Bryn Mawr College, Drew University, Oberlin College, University of California at Berkeley, UCLA, and Vassar College, among others). SIG approaches students in individualized ways in order to serve a variety of abilities, interests, and experiences while attending to social and emotional needs. SIG courses are taught by high-quality instructors who offer innovative, challenging, and fun curricula. Course offerings have included "Exciting Writing," "Fantasy Fiction Fun," "Advertising Smarts—Empowering Young Consumers," "The Writer's Palette," "Word Power," "Comic Book Anthropology," "Word Origins for SAT Success," "Writing Matters," and "Poetry Power."
- *Teen Ink Summer Programs*: http://teenink.com/Summer. This site claims to have the coolest summer opportunities from across the United States and other places in the world

for teens, and it may very well be true. One of the programs is Walnut Hill Summer Writing Institute in Boston and Dublin. It's a 2-week-long summer writing studio that begins with a week outside of Boston, with the second week held in Dublin, Ireland, to study writers Jonathan Swift, James Joyce, and W. B. Yeats. Many other programs are described on the Web site, making this an excellent resource for parents of teens who write.

Internet Resources

In addition to summer and day-long programs, you may find that your child benefits from day-to-day enrichment via the Internet. The Web offers thousands of sites that you can use to bolster your child's interest in writing. A handful are listed and described below.

- *Anthology of Poetry*: http://www.anthologyofpoetry.com. Believing that a child's creation of a poem or short story is a magical event and that writing has the power to transform lives, this forum recognizes writing excellence in students K–12. They select and publish the finest poems and short stories submitted by student writers in soft or hard cover professional anthologies. Purchase of a book is never a factor in the selection process. While this is a classroom-based program, creative parents can inform their children's teachers about it, or can possibly make arrangements to have their children's poetry considered in a homeschool category.
- *Children's Express*: http://www.children's-express.org. The mission of this site is to give young people the power and the means to express themselves publicly on vital issues that

affect them, and in the process, raise their self-esteem and develop their potential. The articles for and about the site's readers are recommended for teenagers, perhaps those in grades 8 and up.

- *Dawn of Day*: http://dawnofday.com. This site may be inspiring to your child and interesting to you, in that it offers writing and illustrating opportunities for online publishing. The writing on the Web site is not formal. However, the opportunities may be helpful if moderated and overseen by you, the parent. Take the time to look at the contents of the Web site, listed along the left side of the page.

- *The Gateway to Education Materials (GEM)* has been combined with *Virtual Reference Desk* and is operated by Syracuse University at http://raven.ischool.washington.edu or http://thegateway.org. This site utilizes a Google-like search master, as well as an incredible glossary through which you can also search. I found multiple high-quality lesson plans, curricula units, interesting articles on the writing process, and appropriate ways to inspire and teach writing to children.

- *Harcourt Achieve*: http://www.harcourtachieve.com. This site is a gold mine for teachers and teaching parents. It includes a comprehensive activity calendar that can inspire children with fresh ideas to write about. Additionally, the Articles and Tips link includes wonderful information and ideas to encourage the writer in your child.

- *HOSTSLink*: http://www.hosts.com. This site offers a free trial to entice you to subscribe to the site. It includes Web-based tools for language arts (LearnerLink) and professional development for early literacy teachers (ProLink).

- *My eCoach & eLibrary*: http://www.my-ecoach.com/elibrary. The educational resources here are copyright friendly. You will find original artwork, photos, educational handouts and templates, literature activities, videos, inquiry-based projects, thematic units, lesson plans, and more—all submitted by teachers. This site includes links to great writing process guides.

- *Kids Online Magazine*: http://www.kidsonlinemagazine. com. This Web site is kid-friendly, with examples of children's writing, tips for writing, contests listed, and opportunities for children to share writing and illustration.
- *Rainbow Bridge*: http://www.summerbridgeactivities.com. This Web site has traditionally focused on helping K–6 children retain and enhance their reading, writing, and math skills over the summer. However, new products now extend the focus to year-round learning, with free resources such as assessment tests by grade level, writing contests, links to information on writing and grammar, and a parent's guide to keeping children busy, happy, and learning during the summer.
- *Scholastic's Writing With Writers Series, Biography Writer's Workshop*: http://teacher.scholastic.com/writewit/biography. This site offers a self-guided opportunity to learn how to write biographical sketches. It provides research and writing strategies, as well as warm-up writing exercises. Students can publish their biographical sketches on this site, as well as read others submitted by students.
- *Scholastic's Writing Workshop: Oral History*: http://teacher. scholastic.com/activities/writing. Scholastic offers a variety of similar Web pages, but the Oral History Workshop page helps teachers guide students through an opportunity to learn more about another person in their family or community as they work step-by-step through the writing process. This site divides the project up into a 3-week schedule, but can be used at a slower or faster pace.

- *SimonSaysKids, Tabs for Teens, and Teachers and Librarians*: http://simonsays.com. Under the SimonSaysKids link you will find, among many great resources, a monthly themed calendar that includes selections of children's literature, and then suggestions for writing and literacy activities based on the literature. In the Teachers and Librarians section you will find downloadable activity kits with age-specific activities, posters, and more.
- *Teaching Ideas for Primary Teachers*: http://www.teachingideas. co.uk/english/creative.htm. This site has curricular aids and ideas for writing units. Click on the Home link for ideas in areas other than writing.
- *Telecollaborate.net*: http://telecollaborate.net. This site helps teachers or parents design or participate in collaborative projects with colleagues from around the globe. Site tools include links to K–12 projects, live classroom conferencing, and technology volunteers. This site truly makes the world our classroom, by guiding the child, teacher, and parent step-by-step to selecting a project and becoming involved. The incredible learning opportunities available here can change the nature of learning, and enthuse your child to see himself as a global learner.
- *Today in Literature*: http://www.todayinliterature.com. Original biographical stories about authors throughout history are posted on this site daily. These fresh biographical sketches are highly browseable, and allow the reader to delve deeply into people, writings, and events in literary history.
- *The Writers Corner*: http://www.writerscorner.com. This site is a community of writers who collaborate and learn together, sharing and honing writing skills. There is a link for a Kids' Writing Center that encourages the exploration

of specific genres, an online writing den, and opportunities to share work for receiving mentorship. There are news feeds and features with tips about improving your writing, as well as online writing references and tools. Registration is free, making this site a great deal.

Contests

Competition is not a universal motivator. However, for the motivation that a contest can offer to some children, and for the teaching opportunities that are inherent in contest guidelines and criteria, you may determine that a contest would be a positive, supporting experience for your child. Select contests sparingly, based on the true interests and passions of your child. Be sure to closely follow the entrance guidelines that are unique and specific to each contest. The experience of shaping their writing according to specifications will help children to shape their aspirations to personal and unique priorities.

- *Laws of Life Essay Contest*: http://lawsoflife.org. The Laws of Life essay contest emphasizes reflection and writing by encouraging students to think about the people and experiences that have helped to shape their values. It challenges them to take a stand for what they believe in. Unlike most essay contests, this one doesn't tell young people what to write about. There is no prescribed topic students have to address. They just have to write from their heart.
- *National Academic League*: http://www.nationalacademic league.org. This competition treats thinking as a sport, combining competitiveness, strategy, team play, and cooperation with critical thinking, problem solving, and scholarship. Schools join the league and play an academic season. Each

game consists of standard-based questions in math, language arts, science, and social studies. Students in grades 5–12 can participate.

- *National History Day contests*: http://nationalhistoryday.org. National History Day contests challenge students in grades 6–12 to produce an exhibit, a video documentary, a paper, or a performance that brings history to life. The national winner receives $1,000. There are also special prizes for African American history, rural history, cryptology, and more. Each state has its own deadlines, with the national competitions held at the University of Maryland each June. State competition deadlines vary in preparation for the national competition. See the Web site for details and guidelines.
- *Scholastic's Writing Awards*: http://www.scholastic.com/ artandwritingawards. On this Web site, you will find information for the writing awards, open to students in grades 7–12 in public, private or parochial school, and homeschooled students in the U.S., its territories, U.S. sponsored schools abroad, and similar schools in Canada. Check in October for current entry information and deadlines. Entry forms can be completed online and printed. The writing categories include dramatic script, humor, journalism, novel writing (winner works with a professional editor to complete the manuscript with possible publication opportunities), personal essay, poetry (single or collection), science fiction and fantasy, short story, short short story, and general writing portfolios. Two contests for writing portfolios are open to students graduating in the year of the contest. Three hundred writing awards are presented each year to winners at the national level, including cash, scholarships, certificates, and publishing and expedition opportunities.

Resources for Researching Writing Ideas

A truly exhaustive list of resources is not feasible in this setting. However, you may find it helpful to follow the links you find in the following sites to other links, creating a chain of support and encouragement for your young writer.

- *Scholastic*: http://www.scholastic.com/kids. This site includes games, contest information, resources, and a variety of links for ideas and activities.
- *Barnes & Noble Sparknotes*: http://www.sparknotes.com. This site offers learners of all ages free study guides on topics ranging from astronomy, to math, to economics, as well as literature, drama, and poetry. You can set up a Sparknotes account to access hundreds of study guides and message boards. Some guides have MP3-audio versions.

Conclusion
Writing and Flying

Many historians and engineers explain the unique success of Orville and Wilbur Wright by recognizing that the brothers confronted the problem of human flight as first a dream and then as a conceivable concept. They approached flight as a puzzle with three distinct component problems: *lift, control,* and *propulsion.* These are also three subproblems of the ideal vision of encouraging our children on their journey as authors. In a very real sense, good parenting and good teaching are like flying. We strive for lift, control, and propulsion. And, we know when we have achieved it.

The Wright Brothers sought the truth that was already available. There were others experimenting with human flight at the turn of the century, and the brothers read everything they could about what was known and what was being tried. Then they approached their own dream of flight with fervent passion. Orville told a friend, "Isn't it astonishing that all those secrets have been preserved for so many years just so that we could discover them!" (Freeman, 1994, p. 66).

As parents, our missions include leading our children to truths. To do this well, we must learn all we can, and then approach our dream with fervent passion. We are privileged to raise marvelous human beings, and it is our job to help them assimilate and accommodate knowledge they are acquiring with new skills, experiences, and wisdom.

Lift

Lift happened for the Wrights because they functioned with synergistic power—that wonderful phenomena where the outcome is greater than the sum of its parts. Orville and Wilbur were nearly inseparable as they grew up. Some said they were more alike than twins, although they were 4 years apart in age. Individually, Wilbur had a visionary nature and was fascinated by the big picture . . . the dream. Orville liked taking things apart, figuring out how they worked, and putting them back together. I tend to favor Wilbur's nature, and I have friends and siblings who share Orville's tendencies. Both types of enthusiasm were critical to the Wright brothers' success, and the same is true in our quests for raising gifted, caring young writers.

Neither of the brothers is given more credit than the other for their discoveries and success. What they each contributed became greater because they were a team. That they both knew all of the component parts of their planes, that they both knew each step of every experiment, and that either one of them could skillfully fly the planes was critical to their later success in bringing flight to Europe and America at roughly the same time.

Synergy soars. It does in classrooms and it does in our homes. Our children get the benefit of our love and our knowledge, and become better writers because of it. The synergy we share between us generates the capabilities of our children to surpass our own. Synergy in parenting and mentoring is a reciprocal and transforming power. It can take us out of ourselves and return us to ourselves as changed selves. That is lift.

A Control System

Through their early glider experiments, the Wrights learned that they could control flight. They first developed wing-warping, and eventually a front rudder, manned and then unmanned. Next, they discovered how to stabilize turns by adding a tail, then making the tale movable, and later, allowing the pilot to control the tail. Over the next 2 years, Orville and Wilbur flew, practicing and gaining skill in turning, ascending at will, and descending gracefully. No success or failure was considered the end of it all, but rather, inspired more experiments leading to more achievements.

When education really makes a difference, the magic is a teacher, who is first a learner and second a guide, who does not stop until he has led others to learning. Children taught and nurtured by loving, energetic parents come to know that the power felt in their writing achievements came only in part from the accumulation of new knowledge and skill. When children become excited about learning and achieving, the reason is not the skill and knowledge, but the mentor, as well.

Children taught and nurtured by loving, energetic parents come to know that the power felt in their writing achievements came only in part from the accumulation of new knowledge and skill.

The exhilaration and enlightenment that entice our children to become engaged writers come from loving examples who are exhilarated and enlightened.

What I have learned about mentoring writers has come from observing my children and students, studying the topic of writing, trying new things, practicing what has worked, and reflecting on all of the above. I've learned how to warp wings, and continually improve control with the addition of my own rudders, new engines, and propellers. You can, too.

After a miserable summer in 1901, Wilbur and Orville closed their camp at Kill Devil Hill sooner than they had planned, and left for home discouraged and dejected. Wilbur wrote,

> We doubted that we would ever resume our experiments. When we looked at the time and money which we had expended, and considered the progress made and the distance yet to go, we considered our experiments a failure. At this time I made the prediction that man would sometime fly, but that it would not be in our lifetime. (as cited in Freeman, 1994, p. 44)

As a teacher I have made mistakes. As a parent I have made ghastly mistakes. I have berated myself and cried my eyes out over them. But, I am trying to learn from my mistakes. Parenting and teaching are both endless cycles of trial and error. Discouragement and failures prompted the Wright Brothers to go home and build their own wind tunnel to create improved calculations. They fashioned wings out of every imaginable material, in every imaginable shape and size and tested them in their wind tunnel. The testing was tedious, repetitive, and painstaking. But, to them it was absorbing. Orville wrote, "Wilbur and I could hardly wait for morning to come to get at something that interested us. That's happiness" (Freeman, 1994, p. 48). That's what learning to write ought to be like, for our children and for us.

Propulsion

The Wright Brothers were really flying once they created their own gasoline engine, light enough and powerful enough to propel their plane, and then designed a propeller based on what they had learned about curved wings. We know when we have propulsion—when things are clicking along, light enough and powerful enough, that we actually gain a sense that the work in which our children are engaged has become their own. Their engines of fascination are of our and their own unique design. We get used to the air up there, and we enjoy a little acceleration, or occasional gliding, because we know how to land.

What our children perceive during propulsion is that we have respect for who they are and what they can become, that we want to know their personal truth, and that we have time for them. They sense when we are trying to see things through their eyes, and that there is room for them to take off on their own. They come to believe that there is a clear road map to success here, and that we have shared it with them. Because they are our children, we care enough to build intellectual shelters in our homes. When our children knock on the door, we let them in and close the door. We wrap them snugly in the warmth of our love and time for them and our belief in them. We lead them to the window, and together we gaze at the world of what could be, what should be, and what can be in their futures.

> ... if they propose to be great writers, they must think and work harder than they mean to, achieve more than they thought they could, and come to believe that good writing involves effort, risk, and personal triumph.

Writing is hard work. Our young writers must come to realize that it is. And, if they propose to be great writers, they must think and work harder than they mean to, achieve more than they thought they could, and come to believe that good writing involves effort, risk, and personal triumph. Our job is to help them create a flight plan that works.

Finally, the Wright Brothers had some sense of how their work was changing the world. I think they'd be blown away by how it has continued to change us. Our ultimate success as parents and mentors can't really be measured until after they have left us. If, on their continuing flight, our children can safely land, in spite of the storms, the setbacks, the delays, and the disappointments—then we can claim to have taught them well. Have a great flight!

References

Arnheim, R. (1989). *Thoughts on art education.* Los Angeles: Getty Center for Education in the Arts.

Bruner, J. (1966). *The process of education.* Cambridge, MA: Harvard University Press.

Calkins, L. M. (2000). *The art of teaching writing.* Boston: Allyn & Bacon.

College Board. (2003). *The neglected "R": The need for a writing revolution.* New York: Author.

Cramer, R. L. (2001). *Creative power: The nature and nurture of children's writing.* New York: Longman.

de Saint-Exupery, A. (1971). *The little prince.* New York: Harcourt Brace Jovanovich.

Ehrlich, E., & DeBruhl, M. (1996). *The international thesaurus of quotations.* New York: HarperCollins Publishers.

Fletcher, R. (1993). *What a writer needs.* Portsmouth, NH: Heinemann.

Fletcher, R., & Portalupi, J. (2001). *Writing workshop: The essential guide.* Portsmouth, NH: Heinemann.

Fox, M. (1992). *Dear Mem Fox, I have read all your books even the pathetic ones: And other incidents in the life of a children's book author.* New York: Harcourt.

Fox, M. (1993). *Radical reflections: Passionate opinions on teaching, learning, and living.* New York: Harcourt.

Freeman, R. (1994). *The Wright brothers: How they invented the airplane.* New York: Holiday House.

Graves, D. (1994). *A fresh look at writing.* Portsmouth, NH: Heinemann.

Heard, G. (1995). *Writing toward home: Tales and lessons to find your way.* Portsmouth, NH: Heinemann.

Hughes, L. (1958). *Notes of a native son.* Retrieved November 6, 2005, from http://www.nytimes.com/books/98/03/29/specials/baldwin-native.html

King, S. (2000). *On writing: A memoir of the craft.* New York: Scribner.

Lamott, A. (1995). *Bird by bird.* New York: Bantam.

Mirriam-Goldberg, C. (1999). *Write where you are: How to use writing to make sense of your life: A guide for teens.* Minneapolis, MN: Free Spirit Publishing.

Murray, D. (1985). *A writer teaches writing: A complete revision* (2nd ed.). Boston: Houghton Mifflin College Division.

Murray, D. (2003). *A writer teaches writing* (Rev. ed.). Boston: Heinle.

NCTE. (September 2005). Good writing instruction is what's needed. *The Council Chronicle*, p. 1.

Nagin, C., & National Writing Project. (2003). *Because writing matters: Improving student writing in our schools.* Hoboken, NJ: Jossey-Bass.

National Writing Project. (2005). *Supporting good writing instruction.* Retrieved September, 29, 2005, from http://www.writingproject.org/encourage/supporting.csp

Paolini, C. (2005). *Dragon tales*. Retrieved October 12, 2005, from http://www.alagaesia.com

Piaget, J. (1955). *The language and thought of the child*. New York: Meridian Books.

Ray, K. W. (1999). *Wondrous words: Writers and writing in the elementary classroom*. Portsmouth, NH: Heinemann.

Ray, K. W. (2002). *What you know by heart: How to develop curriculum for your writing workshop*. Portsmouth, NH: Heinemann.

Russell, D. L. (2005). *Literature for children: A short introduction* (5th ed.). Boston: Pearson/Allyn & Bacon.

Sabine, G., & Sabine, P. (1983). *Books that made the difference: What people told us*. Hamden, CT: Shoe String Press.

Spandel, V. (2005a). *The 9 rights of every writer: A guide for teachers*. Portsmouth, NH: Heinemann.

Spandel, V. (2005b). *Creating writers through 6-trait writing* (4th ed.). Boston: Pearson/Allyn & Bacon.

Spinelli, J. (1998). *Knots in my yo-yo string*. New York: Random House Children's Books.

Vygotsky, L. (1962). *Thought and language*. Cambridge, MA: M.I.T. Press.

Walton, R. (2003). *How I came to write language arts picture books*. Retrieved October 29, 2005, from http://www.rickwalton.com/rickpub/langarts.htm

Wasserstein, P. (1995). What middle schoolers say about their schoolwork. *Educational Leadership, 53*(1), 41–43.

About the Author

Nancy Peterson believes that literacy can empower children. Nancy frequently gives presentations on elementary language arts methods and building strengths in children. She also consults with former students as they set up writing workshops in their own classrooms, helping children become writers. Nancy loves reading children's literature and watching movies in the second row at the theater. She currently serves as an associate professor of teacher education and as the Faculty Service-Learning Coordinator at Utah Valley State College. Nancy holds an Ed.D. in elementary education with minors in gifted education and counseling education from the University of Virginia.